On the left, enclosed in flames, is the Supreme Deity of the volcanic island of Bali. This was the primitive origin of the idea of an "angel" and is what geologists today call a "lava bomb," which is a large rock ejected by a volcano. *Photo by author.*

The Invention of God

☼

The Natural Origins of Mythology and Religion

Bill Lauritzen

Grateful acknowledgment is made to the National Geographic Society,
NOAA, and the Volcanological Survey of Indonesia for permission to
include certain photos and maps.

Library of Congress Cataloging-in-Publication Data

Lauritzen, Bill, 1951-

The Invention of God: The Origins of Religious and Scientific Thought by
Bill Lauritzen

Includes bibliographical references.

ISBN 0-9787543-3-6
Second Edition

  1. Science. 2. Religion. 3. Mythology. 4. Ancient History. 4.
      Philosophy. 5. Geology.

I. Title

Front and Back Cover Design: Michael Lujan.
Cover Photo: Eruption of the "anak Krakatau," 2008 by Thomas Schiet.

Dedicated to

My Parents

My Teachers at:
Shelby School
Maercker School
Hinsdale Jr. High
Hinsdale Central High School
U.S. Air Force Academy
Purdue University

The courageous souls
Who choose to write
What they observed,
And whose insights
Shaped our culture.

The word 'religion' comes from the Latin for 'binding together,' to connect that which has been sundered apart ... And in this sense of seeking the deepest interrelations among things that superficially appear to be sundered, the objectives of religion and science, I believe, are identical or very nearly so.

Carl Sagan, The Gifford Lectures

Contents

The Invention of God

☼

Preface ☼

As we stood at the base of one of the world's most deadly volcanoes, our guides tried to talk us out of going any farther. The language was difficult to understand, but the message was clear. They had just brought us across a five-hour stretch of ocean in an old fishing boat, but they knew that to go farther was to risk their own lives as well as ours.

Ahead, there were no plants or animals. Just boulders and rocks. Scattered here and there amidst the boulders were vents, emitting poisonous sulfur gas from inside the volcano.

This dragon was sleeping now, but a few years ago, it had taken the lives of several Americans. Just over 100 years ago, in a fit of rage, it exploded and the resulting tidal wave killed more than 36,000 people.

Our small expedition was composed of two Dutch, two Danish, two French, and myself, the American. I had chartered the boat from a small fishing village to the North and managed to gather the others to help with the cost. We all hesitated for a moment at the guides' warnings, and then four of us went on without the guides or the others. The guides knew there was nothing they could do to stop us, but they told us to be back in an hour, probably hoping to minimize our exposure to the volcano.

In the heat of the equatorial Sun, we hiked up the lunar-like terrain...

It was a hazy day in Indonesia. A five month long drought had created dangerous conditions. Forest fires raged on the island of Sulawesi to the East, and the trade winds blew the smoke into the Sunda strait where we were exploring. Farther north, in Sumatra, people were wearing scarves over their faces. In less than a week, I

1

would be flying south to Java, while a jet going north would crash, killing all on board. I suspect that the haze was partly responsible.

Meanwhile, as we climbed the side of the volcano, I could see through the haze to an island in the distance. That island was what was left of 1882 Krakatau, before the explosion in 1883. The island, two-thirds of it now missing, had stretched across the waters to where we now stood. Most of the original Krakatau had been blown into the sky, part of it raining down on the surrounding countryside, part of it remaining suspended in the upper atmosphere where it would affect sunsets and weather around the world for the next several years. The "child of Krakatau," anak Krakatau, on which we were standing, would rise above the ocean in 1927, after 45 years. It was a volcanic resurrection of the kind that had happened many times and in many places throughout the world, and would have a huge influence on mythology and religion.

We walked on a slippery, gray, sandy-like mixture of dust and ash that had been expelled from the volcano. Now and then, we stopped to look at the lava bombs. These were rocks of various sizes that had been thrown out of the crater of the volcano. As they landed, they made their own little craters. Most were small enough to lift. However, we stopped to examine one the size of small Volkswagen that the volcano recently had coughed up.

I was beginning to feel a little uneasy. We took some photos and I again noticed the large expanse of sea separating us from the remains of Krakatau. I wondered how much my companions knew about this volcano. I explained to them how it had exploded in 1883 and pointed out to them where the island once had stood.

We stopped to examine the white sulfur compounds around one of the many vents that led down into the interior of the cone. I took some pictures. The eerie silence combined with the smoking vents and large lava bombs eventually began to get to me. I recommended we turn back before we reached the summit. The rest agreed without much discussion. Perhaps they too were feeling uneasy.

We headed back to the mainland of Sumatra from the child of Krakatau. The noise from the boat's engine was deafening, and I had somehow lost the earplugs that I bought in a travel store in Los Angeles.

The Earth continued its rotation and the sea reached up and kissed the home star. A calm settled over the boat despite the loud "chug, chug, chug." I moved to the front where one of the young guides was perched on the bow, staring ahead. Unlike we Europeans and Americans, the guides had wisely worn their oldest and most tattered clothing.

Looking at the face of the guide, I saw a deep sense of satisfaction. It occurred to me then that the volcano held the same fascination for him as it did for me. Perhaps it has been the same for every human, since Homo erectus *looked on it about 2 million years ago.*

I had an urge to continue on in that boat through the Sunda Strait. To follow the coastline of Sumatra, and then Burma, and then India. And then beyond India, to the coast of Arabia, and the Red Sea and Egypt. Some primitive instinct was taking over my psyche, some deep personal desire to know the truth. "Follow the coast," it said, "Follow the coast ..."

To rid ourselves of religion, we need to understand how it started. I have found that all the religions of the world, despite their multifaceted outward manifestations, originally emerged from the same natural phenomena: 1) The Heavens Above Us (astronomical phenomena), 2) The Earth Below Us (volcanoes and other geological phenomena), and 3) The Air Around Us (oxygen, or which early humans called by various names such as "spirit," "psyche," "ba," "prana," "reiki," "qi," and "tao").

This book will deal with 2 and 3, since 1, astronomical phenomena, has been dealt with so extensively and it's influence on mythology and religion is largely known (after all, it is called the Heavens), while the influence of geology and oxygen have remained relatively unknown by the general public.

I think most ministers, priests, rabbis, mullahs, monks, and who claim knowledge of ancient sacred texts are ignorant of the true meaning of these texts or else hiding this meaning. Thus, to some degree, their legitimacy must be questioned. Even scholars such as Joseph Campbell and Carl Jung, who have tried to understand and explain mythology and religion, missed these fundamental sources. Campbell and Jung both overlaid psychological explanations on top of purely natural phenomena, such as volcanic explosions, volcanic resurrections, lava lakes, magma, and the biospheric recycling of oxygen, and thereby hid these vital phenomena.

In this book, I suggest that the geological and volcanic catastrophes and resurrections in an area of the Indian Ocean near Indonesia, and elsewhere in the world, were important in forming our religions and mythologies. In the late 1990s, I predicted future catastrophes in the Indian Ocean. Little did I realize that only a few years later my prediction would come true with the deaths of 225,000 in a tsunami.

This book in not meant to be an exhaustive survey of all the world's myths or religions.[1] I have picked the more prominent religions and myths, and I rely at times on the surveys of others. I avoid a tedious tome, full of "laundry lists" of supporting evidence in favor of a clear outline of the theory. Even a casual perusal of the literature, after examining this book, will reveal much more evidence. On the other hand, if at times the book does seem too tedious for you, feel free to skip ahead.

From a historical perspective, this book is just the latest in a series of discoveries that show the mysteries of life to be known, physical entities. For millennia, it was thought that some *élan vital* or "life force" made living things different from mere matter. Thanks to people like van Leeuwenhoek, Lavoisier, Pasteur, Hooke, Harvey, Copernicus, Galileo, Newton, Kepler, Einstein, Cuvier, Darwin, Mendel, Mendeleev, Norbert Weiner, James Watson and Francis Crick, and others, this idea has slowly changed. There *is* "a vital immaterial spirit," but what you will see is that this "spirit" is largely explainable with modern chemistry.

David Sloan Wilson has said, "What before was a jumble of uninterpretable facts suddenly becomes organized by the relationships made reasonable by the theory."[2] This book will shine light on many previously dark areas. *My goal is to present the overarching theory, as stated above, and give a reasonable amount of evidence for it.*

I shall be giving evidence for some surprising and interesting findings that support this theory. Here are some:

The "battles between the Gods" represented in various myths are ancient observations of volcanic lightning interacting with volcanic eruption.

The periodic major eruptions of Krakatau and Thera and other volcanoes led to early ideas of resurrection, the Osiris--Horus resurrection, the Phoenix, and the Ouroboros.

The Great Pyramid, and most other pyramids, represent a volcano.

Early humans connected the light in the heavens, by way of lightning, to the light and fire they saw on earth, in a grand unification theory of fire-earth-air-water.

Preface

What the early humans called "psyche," "spirit," "soul," "ba," "reiki," "qi or chi," "tao," "prana," "universal energy," or "ruach" was an attempt to describe and understand what we now know as "oxygen."

Magic, religion, mythology, alchemy, chemistry, and science all to go back to a common beginning: the observation of the natural world of the heavens, volcanoes, and the atmosphere.

Of course, there are myths concerned with other things than the Earth, the air, and the heavens. How a woman gave birth (through the sperm of a man) was probably a mystery for many millennia. However, I believe the myths I discuss here are the most spectacular, mysterious, powerful, and pervasive.

Although I am quite confident of my general findings, at times I speculate beyond my data. I feel this is my prerogative as a writer, and I realize some of these speculations may prove false. However, I try to speculate in a rational and responsible manner. *Remember that the most extravagant speculations are those that claim "supernatural" powers and events!* The speculations I make are realistic, tame and quite credible in comparison. The burden of proof lies on those who claim *extra*ordinary events, not with those who logically interpret historical religious and mythological writings considering natural phenomena.

Who should read this book? Anyone who is intellectually courageous. Anyone who wants some clarity on some of the fundamental questions of our age. Anyone who wants to understand the beginnings of religion and science. This book could be used in a class on critical thinking, comparative religions, anthropology, psychology or the history of science and religion. It could be used as the basis to clarify translations from ancient tongues. This book also could be used to combat religious dogma, wherever it might appear: East, West or Middle East.

I have a hope, but it is not the hope of an "afterlife," which is promised by many religions. It is the hope that by using logic, rationality and the scientific method, we can overcome the difficult survival problems that lie ahead of us. One if these problems, we shall see, is the coming eruption of a super-volcano.

I also hope that this book can counterbalance the constant barrage of propaganda and advertisements that we receive daily from commercial, religious and political sources. As you know, these communications do not always have our best interests at heart.

Preface

Ninety percent of this work was finished in the late 1990s. I tried getting these ideas published as articles in various journals and magazines in 1997, but I think due to their multidisciplinary nature, was unsuccessful. So, in 1999, I put them on my web site to start some discussion.

So join me on a journey into the ancient past—into an age when there were no separate branches of knowledge. In fact, there were not even words such as "religion" or "science." We will follow the Tree of Knowledge back through geology, chemistry, and alchemy to the trunk of the tree, where we will examine some of the most "sacred" stories in the world. One final warning: you may find some of what you read here disturbing. I did. However, think of it as a cold bath: you may not like it, but you will come out of it feeling greatly refreshed.

Egypt is where we will begin our journey. In my search for truth, I delved deeply into the mythological writings of the Nile River civilization. I was completely stunned by what I discovered, and my view of ancient history and religion was permanently altered.

Usage Notes:

1) There is a glossary of some basic volcanic terms at the end of the book. The most important thing to know at this point is that *magma* is beneath the ground and when it emerges, it is known as *lava*.

2) At times I spell "earth" with a capital ("Earth") to emphasize the more modern, planetary view.

3) In order not to express any favoritism among various religions or mythologies, I shall always capitalize the word God and Gods.

3) I use the term "early humans" often, and by this I generally mean prehistorical, that is, before about 5,000 years ago, going back to...who knows how far? Perhaps even as far as *Homo erectus*? There is some evidence suggesting that humans had symbolic thoughts of an afterlife as long as 350,000 years ago. However, 50,000 years ago a fundamental increase in our brain's capacity seems to have appeared, perhaps due to a genetic mutation.

4) At times I use two words or a hyphenated word, instead of the more common compound word to emphasize a point.

5) When discussing ancient Egyptian hieroglyphs I mostly use the Budge translations, as these are most readily available to the average reader.

6) I suggest you supplement this book with photos, maps and diagrams from the Internet, which are readily available nowadays.

7) I apologize for any typos. We have done our best to eliminate them. Please email me at my web site if you find any.

1 ☼

The Pharaohs' Volcanoes

If we examine the popular literature concerning Ancient Egypt, we find a plethora of books with unsubstantiated claims of a bizarre and speculative nature. Alien visitations, past lives, flying machines, genetic manipulation, nuclear power, acoustical power, Martian visitation, etc., are some common themes. A recent book explains that Egyptian religion describes an exploding planet between Mars and Jupiter.[3]

The more serious scholars of mythology and religion, often tucked away in their ivory towers, at various universities, expound in learned tomes regarding the meaning of myth. Carl Jung and Joseph Campbell express theories regarding the "collective unconscious," or the "hero's journey." Schools such as structuralism and modern psychoanalysis spew forth, in endless streams, various convoluted interpretations.

What about the scientist? Often blinded by compartmentalization, he or she continues on the tradition of previous researchers. Modern Egyptologists still recycle the century-old story that Nile Valley hunter-gatherers were for some reason obsessed with magical and seemingly incomprehensible chants to guide the newly dead person into an abstract heaven with abstract Gods (quite similar to some modern religions).

Rare indeed is the scientist who breaks free of the walls surrounding his or her particular department and attempts to look elsewhere. However, they do exist.

In 1939, Sigmund Freud wrote *Moses and Monotheism* in

7

which he states that "Jahve," or Jehovah, was probably a volcano-god originally. In 1969, Oxford scholar J. V. Luce stated that certain passages in Hesiod's *Theogony* could "be interpreted as a classic description of a volcanic eruption." In 1973, Indiana University scholar, Dorothy Vitaliano, in *Legends of the Earth: Their Geological Origins*, strengthened the connection between geology and mythology, when she coined the term "geomythology."

Finally, in 1992, Mott Greene, a MacArthur Foundation Fellow, continued on where Luce left off, and gave a detailed analysis of "Hesiod's Volcanoes." His most important contribution was bringing Zeus solidly within the field of natural phenomenon by linking him with what is called "volcanic lightning." This was a very important contribution that I will discuss shortly.

For my part, I poured over ancient hieroglyphs for months and months and searched through used bookstores and university libraries for obscure and ancient texts. In this chapter and the next, I give a summary of this research that led me to an astonishing and unexpected conclusion: *that the Great Pyramids represent volcanoes.* Though perhaps this is not so astonishing when you realize that at least some etymologists believe this word (pyro + mid), means "fire in the middle."[4]

In this book, I purposely ignore the mathematical and astronomical correlations that have been claimed for the Great Pyramids. Other books and articles have discussed these in detail, and some interesting correlations undoubtedly exist. However, let the reader beware. For example, Dr. E. C. Krupp has effectively debunked the supposed alignment of the Great Pyramids with the constellation Orion.[5]

The Nile River Valley

If we follow the Nile River upstream, we progress through all of ancient Egypt. We cross upward into the Sudan, the land of the ancient Kush. We progress through Khartoum, where the Nile has split into its two main branches, the Blue Nile and the White Nile. The White Nile flows from Uganda and the Blue Nile from Ethiopia. It is hard for some people to visualize this on the map. The Nile flows from the South, so as one goes further south one is going *up* into the highlands and mountains of central Africa.

Either way we go, we eventually run into numerous volcanoes, which are the result of the Great Rift Valley. This geological formation spans most of Eastern Africa and is one of the most prominent geological features on the planet. Its origin is not fully understood even today.

In Tanzania, this rifting system forms the high volcano Kilimanjaro, which may someday erupt again. In Ethiopia, the rift spawns many volcanoes, including island-volcanoes of Lake Turkana. It continues on into the Red Sea where there are several more island volcanoes. Meanwhile, in Zaire (on the border of Uganda), are the volcanic Virunga Mountains. (These mountains are famous as the home of the mountain gorilla.)

This Rift Valley is well known for supplying archeologists with human and pre-human fossils. Here we find Olduvai Gorge, made famous by Lewis and Mary Leakey; here we find Lake Turkana, where their son, Richard Leakey, helped find "Turkana Boy"; here we find Hadar, where Don Johanson found "Lucy."

Ancient hominids probably migrated northward to the Middle East, either by following the Nile downward, crossing the Sahara during a "wetter" period between ice ages or following the coastline of Africa northward. There were probably multiple migrations.[6] In any case, these ancient people eventually arrived in what we now call the Nile River Valley or Egypt, bringing with them their ancient beliefs and knowledge.

On the walls of some of the pyramids and temples, on the coffins of the nobles and on various papyri, are the most ancient religious writings in the world. So although not properly books or texts, these writings have been compiled into texts which are called the "Pyramid Texts," the "Coffin Texts," the "Book of the Dead," and others. Of course, they did not call them "religious" writings—they had no word for "religion." They were their science.

It is true that many references within these materials are extremely difficult to understand. However, let us assume instead that Nile River people were influenced by ancient observations of volcanoes and other geological phenomena. Do the hieroglyphs now make more sense? In this chapter, I put forth the thesis that the pyramids were imitations of volcanoes, and the Pharaoh was put inside the pyramid to be joined with Osiris, God of the Underworld.

Anthropologist Brian Fagan proposed that climate change was the reason people moved out of Africa:

> Oceans and deserts are powerful engines in human affairs.
> The Sahara is another enormous pump, fueled by constant
> atmospheric changes and global climate shifts. For tens of
> thousands of years its arid wastes isolated the very first

anatomically modern humans from the rest of the world. But some 130,000 years ago, the Sahara received more rainfall than today. The desolate landscape supported shallow lakes and semi-arid grasslands. The desert sucked in human populations from the south, then pushed them out to the north and west. The Saharan pump brought *Homo sapiens sapiens* into Europe and Asia. And from there they had spread all over the globe . . .. But the pump shut down again. As glacial cold descended on northern latitudes, the desert dried up once more, forming a gigantic barrier between tropical Africa and the Mediterranean world. Fifteen thousand years ago, global warming brought renewed rainfall to the Sahara. The pump came to life again. Foragers and then cattle herders flourished on the desert's open plains and by huge shallow lakes, including a greatly enlarged Lake Chad. Then, as the desert dried up after 6000 B.C., the pump closed again, with its last movements pushing its human populations out to the Sahel, where they live today. Like the North Atlantic Oscillation, the Sahara is a pump with the capacity to change human history.[7]

This idea is known as the "Saharan Pump Hypothesis." Let us assume it is correct for a minute. We know that early Africans lived along the huge volcanic rift area, where many of the world's finest human fossils have been found. As the Africans were sucked into the Sahara and then pushed out into Europe and Asia, they certainly would have brought stories of the fantastic volcanoes with them. Coming down the Nile toward the Mediterranean, farther and farther away from the volcanoes (and their God?), they would have wanted to preserve this knowledge. The pyramids were the attempt. The pyramids would represent these ancient volcanoes. However, many other geological areas also could have influenced or reinforced their beliefs.

We shall see that volcanoes in the sea have importance for Egyptian myths. Thera (Santorini) is a volcanic island that has been singled out as a possible influence on Egyptian events, including the "Exodus.[8] My research shows that it has exploded many times in the past. [My comments will be in brackets.]

Santorini is a complex of overlapping shield volcanoes...Some of the cliff is thought to be a caldera wall associated with an eruption 21,000 years ago. Druitt and Francaviglia (1992) found evidence of at least 12 large explosive eruptions in the last 200,000 years at Santorini [Thera]. [That's about one massive eruption every 17,000 years.] The white layer at the top is the Minoan tephra from the 1,650 B.C. eruption.[9]

Volcanic Areas Possibly Influencing Ancient Egyptians
The African Rift Valley: the Virunga Range, Kilimanjaro, Ethiopia volcanoes, and Red Sea volcanoes, volcanic islands of Lake Turkana
Volcanoes of Indonesia (Krakatau)
Volcanic Islands of the Eastern Atlantic (Azores, Canary, and Cape Verde)
Volcanoes of Iceland
Mediterranean Volcanoes such as Thera (Santorini)
Volcanoes of Italy (Etna, Vesuvius, Stromboli, Volcano, Kameno Vouno, etc.)
Volcanoes of the volcanic island arc of the Caribbean

Although I am quite confident of my findings, the topic deserves extended research. I have surveyed much, but not all Egyptian hieroglyphs. Mostly, I have used the "Book of the Dead," since this is readily available. Further research would include a complete analysis of all these volcanoes along with an attempt to match them with Nile River hieroglyphs. In addition, further analysis of the ancient patterns of ocean trading and ocean migration is needed.

I visited several volcanoes, but not in Africa. My first was the Hawaiian volcano, Kilauea. It was here that I saw new land being formed before my eyes, and choked on the noxious smell of sulfur compounds so typical of volcanoes.

In Indonesia, I climbed the active volcano, child of Krakatau, in the Sunda Strait, between Java and Sumatra. Here, I saw a new island ecosystem forming as the island rises up from the seabed to replace its Killer Parent. That parent was Krakatau, which, exploded in 1883 and caused 36,000 deaths.

I also climbed Mount Merapi, on Java, which erupts fairly regularly every 20-30 minutes (at least in 1997), as if the Earth had a heartbeat. A massive explosion of this volcano about 1,000 years ago probably caused the collapse of the civilization in central Java then. From the air, I saw the entire string of volcanoes from Bali up into Southern Sumatra.

In addition, I studied many photographs and accounts of various volcanoes and their eruptions or explosions. I learned to love and respect them. They taught me, as I believe they taught early humans.

Grand Unification Theory of Ancient Humans

When Thomas Kuhn wrote his classic work, *The Structure of Scientific Revolutions*, he wondered how Aristotle, a brilliant thinker, could have been so wrong about some things. In a flash of insight, he realized that he should look at the world through Aristotle's eyes.[10] So let us try to do what Kuhn did, look at the world as ancient humans might have seen it.

A blind man develops extraordinary powers of hearing. From the sound of someone's footsteps, a blind person frequently can tell the identity of that person. The cutting off of one sense causes the others to become more acutely aware. The ancient humans, having had no telescopes or microscopes, could not see many of the things that we can see, and were in a sense blind. However, they had the same high-capacity brains as we do, and the same powers of observation. They may have been able to see in ways that we have forgotten.

Sources of Light In the Ancient World
Sun
Moon
Stars and Planets
Fire
Lightning
Lava

To consider the minds of early humans, we must imagine a completely different world than our own. A world without electricity. In this world, there were only a few sources of light: the 1) Sun, 2) the Moon, 3) the stars and planets, 4) fire, 5) lightning, and, most importantly for our purposes, 6) lava. Without electricity, these sources had a much greater importance in the lives of people than they have in our world.

To those of us who have never seen a volcano (espeeially at night), perhaps we would never think of lava as a source of light. However, to early man, who may have differentiated (evolved) in the volcanic Great Rift Valley, and could see the continuous glowing at night, this lava-fire-light must have been both attractive and fearsome.

From earliest times man observed the following "strange"

Hieroglyphs from the Book of the Dead.

almost "magical" phenomena: 1) liquid lava-fire turning into solid rock, 2) stone turning into soil, 3) soil turning into greenery, 4) wood and other organic bodies decomposing into the earth, somehow disappearing, seemingly almost "eaten" by the earth, 5) wood and other organic materials (dead bodies, oil) burning to become air and ashes. 6) water disappearing (evaporating) into air, 7) air turning into water (rain), and, much later, 8) metals melting into liquid. We take these things for granted, but sometime try to look at them as if seeing them for the first time.

Here is an example (of number 4) from the "Book of the Dead":

Let not my body become worms, but deliver me as thou didst deliver thyself. I pray thee, let me not fall into rottenness, as thou lettest every god, and every goddess, and every animal, and every reptile, see corruption, when the soul has gone out of them after their death.[11]

From all these observations, the ancient humans formulated the idea (somewhat correct) that the world is made of four basic things: 1) Fire, 2) Earth, 3) Air, 4) Water. They also developed the idea (somewhat correct) that these things could be transformed into one another.

Of course, it is natural to assume that all sources of light are somehow connected. I believe this explains much apparent confusion in the hieroglyphic material. One frequently sees mixtures of various entities. For example, one sees "Osiris-Ra," "Osiris-Horus," and "Osiris-Geb." One sees Seth (or Set), the God of Storms and Disorder, being put into the boat of Ra. Atum is referred to as "Atum-Ra." Alternatively, Osiris is associated with the West, and the setting Sun. Often, the newly dead noble will be linked to a God, as in "Osiris-Ani."

13

Substance	"Magical" change to:	Scientific Reason
Lava or liquid fire	stone	phase change
lava stone	soil	erosive breakdown
Soil	greenery	natural seeding
wood and other organic materials (dead bodies)	the earth	decomposition
wood and other organic material (dead bodies, oil)	air, ashes	burning
water	air	evaporation, boiling
air	water/rain	condensation of water vapor
stone, metals	liquid	phase change by heating

We can see how ancient humans could have imagined these Gods blending with the fire-light that exists beneath the ground as magma. It also explains why sometimes Ra is called the Lord of All. As the essence of Light, he would have been. This then may have been a Grand Unification Theory of Ancient Humans: all things can emerge from fire or light.

The ancient writers of the hieroglyphs saw the Sun, Moon, stars and planets rotate in the sky from east to west and disappear in the West beneath the horizon. Then they saw them reappear in the East. They assumed that during that time they were beneath the earth and were rejuvenated in the underworld, the world of red magma. The red, setting Sun (called Atum) was linked with the red magma and lava.

The "Book of the Dead" says, referring to Ra:

O thou divine substance, from whom all living things came into being ... thou maker of the things that are ... thou hast produced whatsoever cometh forth from the waters ...[12]

The Lava to Soil Breakdown

When in Hawaii, as I mentioned, I visited the live volcano of Kilauea. As the long, thin line of people marched over the black lava terrain toward the rising steam, they were chatting and talking. Upon reaching the volcano, I stood a few feet from the hot lava, as it flowed into the ocean and created rocks and new land before my eyes. I never had as profound an experience as seeing the act of creation of land from liquid lava.

The surf was full of black sand. I entered the water not far from the site to the astonishment of the people around me. I swam as close to the lava as I dared, and putting my head underwater, I could hear what sounded like an anchor chain being lowered, but was the sound of liquid lava hardening into rock as it hit the cool ocean.

On the way back over the lava terrain, the most noticeable and unexpected thing was the solemn quiet of the procession. It reminded me of a church or temple. It appeared everyone was as moved by the experience as I was. Here was a Mecca!

The "Big Island" of Hawaii contains all but one of the fifty-some ecosystems, ranging from tropical rain forest to arctic tundra high on the mountain. I saw rural surroundings identical to those I had seen long ago in Illinois. Gentle, rolling hills covered with corn and threatened with rain. In Hawaii, I first saw the possibilities of lava origins for all landmasses. One current estimate puts this proportion at 80%. In other words, 80% of the landmasses you see around you probably came originally from lava flows.

Basalt lava rock weathers rapidly. Some Hawaiian maps have the dates of the past lava flows printed on them (for example, 1919, 1927, 1974, etc.), and one can see the successive breakdown of these flows by gradual weathering according to the following sequence: 1) liquid magma, 2) lava flows that look like gigantic, instant-frozen, black and purple rapids, 3) large boulders, 4) smaller boulders and rocks and finally, 5) rich, volcanic soil. The older dates, of course, had the most weathering.

Lava to Soil Transformation Sequence
1) liquid magma
2) hardened lava flows that look like gigantic, instant-frozen, black and purple rapids
3) large boulders
4) smaller boulders and rocks
5) rich, fertile soil

The Volcanic Resurrection

The early humans also observed volcanoes in various stages of creation or erosion. For example, on the island of Hawaii, if one starts with the Big Island and moves west through Maui, Lanai, Molokai, Oahu, and Kauai, the islands become older as evidenced by the progressive erosion by wind and ocean, so that while the Big Island (Hawaii) has a peak elevation of 13,800 feet, Kauai has a peak elevation of only 5,200 feet. Eventually Kauai will become just a coral reef and then entirely disappear beneath the sea.

15

Thus, these ancient scientist-priests put together (correctly) the following sequence:
1) lava rising up out of the sea, lake, or land,
2) the lava cooling to become solid rock,
3) the lava rock being slowly worn down into rich, fertile soil,
4) the rich, fertile soil nurturing plants and animals,
5) the volcano eventually being worn down (to a coral island or extinct cone), or the volcano exploding and destroying almost everything around it, and, in many cases,
6) a new volcano rising to replace the old one (as with Santorini and Krakatau).

The Volcano Krakatau

In 1997, I climbed the "child of Krakatau" in the middle of the Sunda Strait. This first appeared above the ocean, amid the remains of the 1883 explosion, in 1927.

Krakatau may have violently erupted as many as 10 or 12 times in the last 950,000 years.[13] Each time this happened, a new volcano then grew in the place of the exploded one.

On the newly formed volcanic island, a lush ecosystem slowly blossomed forth from undifferentiated rock and ash.[14] We can imagine ancient scientist-priests, over thousands of years, observing this establishment of life on Krakatau, Thera, or on volcanoes at other locations in the Mediterranean, Lake Turkana in Africa, the Caribbean, or Iceland.

Modern biologists are extremely interested in seeing how the ecosystem is reestablished on volcanic islands: They ask themselves these questions: What are the first species to arrive? How do they get there? How long does it take them to establish themselves on the island?

However, the ancient humans probably were not aware that life came to exist on this island from the other islands. They might not have seen the arrival of a seed, which was inadvertently carried to the island by a bird. To them it might have seemed as if life *spontaneously* appeared on the volcanic island. It must have seemed as if this were the way that creation itself took place. First, an island rising from the ocean, and then life appearing almost by magic on the island.

Tens of thousands of years or more of observations of volcanoes may have allowed ancient humans to develop a proto-science (quite accurate in some respects) that described for them the creation and destruction of life. To these people, God was the Volcano God. This God lived inside the Earth. In the Nile River Valley civilization, this God was Osiris, God of the Underworld.

Also, the ancient humans saw the huge out-gassing from volcanoes and may have guessed (correctly) that the Earth's atmosphere (Shu) came from the inside of the volcano.

New plant life spreading on the child of Krakatau, 1997. Photo by author.

The Recycling of Life

Observations of astute scientist-priests enabled them also to guess (somewhat correctly) that, besides a lava-soil phase change and a volcanic resurrection, a life *re*cycling also exists. In this cycle:

1) Humans and other animals are born on volcanic rich soil that arose from the depths of the earth.
2) They grow and get their energy from plants in rich lava-soil, or from animals that eat the plants in rich lava-soil,
3) They live out their lives.
4) They die.
5) They decompose (disappear) back into rich lava-soil.
6) They are "reborn" as a new eruption takes place.

Thus, the idea of reincarnation or rebirth may have begun. Actually, this reincarnation (literally "again-body") *does occur* as the biosphere recycles the various elements of the body (oxygen, hydrogen, carbon, nitrogen, etc.) into the soil, atmosphere, etc., and new bodies can then be formed from these elements (as directed by the genetic recipe). Of course embalming or mummification can delay this recycling process.

Unfortunately, reincarnation is popularly misinterpreted so

17

that people think their individual personality is reborn. We now know that the personality is a result of unique genetic and environmental factors. These genetic and environmental factors will never be the same for any two individuals. You are unique.

The Egyptian "Book of the Dead," in which the dead person is given instructions to prepare them for being reborn ("coming forth by day") is a good example of the early thinking about reincarnation. It is also an example of a society trying to ritualize and control this natural process of decay and recycling. (More on this later.)

The ancient humans probably deduced that simple forms of life changed into more complex forms of life. For example, in India it was thought that if one was "good" one could "reincarnate" as a more complex life form.

Species Differentiation

Apparently, a tropical volcanic island makes a wonderful natural laboratory, and the ancient people probably took advantage of this fact. However, volcanic islands inspire even modern scientists.

Alfred Russel Wallace, who, independently of Darwin, derived the theory of species differentiation, was moved to postulate a *choosing or elimination by nature* after visiting Indonesia and seeing its multitudinous life forms. Darwin himself wrote his classic books after seeing the differentiated life forms of the volcanic Galapagos Islands of the South Pacific. In other words, both Darwin and Wallace witnessed the differentiated life forms of tropical, volcanic islands before formulating their ideas on how many species came to exist.

Perhaps the theory might have come earlier, but European thinking then was hampered during the long Dark Ages by a literal interpretation (in other words, misinterpretation) of the Bible, one that still exists today in so-called "fundamentalism." To a people that may have been the first to artificially select certain plants for cultivation and certain plants among those plants, etc., a similar selection/ elimination in their natural surroundings of all life forms would have been an easy idea.

In fact, in ancient Egyptian mythology there was the Divine Potter who formulated humankind out of the mud. Observing the repopulating of the environment after a volcanic eruption or explosion may have been the inspiration. This idea was an early precursor to natural selection.

The Pharaohs' Volcanoes

Atum-Ra

The setting Sun was referred to as Atum or Atum-Ra. This might have been because the Egyptians believed that the Sun traveled through the underworld and emerged in the East at dawn. So, the red setting Sun may have reminded them of red magma beneath the crust.

The Primeval Mound: A Volcanic Creation?

In the creation story of the ancient Nile River Valley civilization, it talks about the First Time: a time in the ancient past when creation occurred. At this time, there existed Primeval Waters that extended in all directions. From out of these Primeval Waters arose the Primeval Mound (also called the First Place or Primeval Throne).

R.T. Rundle Clark, a noted British Egyptologist who wrote during the late 1950s, states that the land is like a "spitting forth" from the waters, or a "spitting serpent," "signifying outflow or exhalation." Look at the following reference:

> O Atum! When you came into being you rose up as a High Hill ... Hail to you, O Becoming One who came into being of himself ... You spat forth as Shu, you expectorated as Tefnut.[15]

Shu is the God of the air. Tefnut is Goddess of moisture, a lioness-goddess, who may represent hardened lava, which can take strange shapes, perhaps like a lion.

Of course, these descriptions are similar to the rising of the child of Krakatau, in 1927, in the Sunda Strait, the rising of Surtsey near Iceland, in 1963.

Along this line, the hieroglyphs mention the Phallus of Ra, which was probably a volcano. A volcano would certainly remind one of a penis. In the 1883 volcanic explosion of Krakatau, the volcano rumbled for months before its final climatic explosion. Here are some quotes from the "Book of the Dead."

> Hail, Phallus of Ra, which advanceth and beateth down opposition. ... the Phallus of Ra [which is] the head of Osiris.[16]

And from the Papyrus of Nebseni,

> Now, he whose mouth shineth and whose head moveth is the phallus of Osiris, but others say it is of Ra.[17]

19

The Cosmic Egg: Underwater Lava Flow?

Where did the Primeval Mound come from? From something called a Cosmic Egg beneath the waters. For many weeks, I made the same mistake that previous scholars have made, and assumed that the writers of the ancient hieroglyphs had merely made up this idea about the Egg.

However, I saw a documentary video, "Volcano Daredevils," about two famous French volcanologists, Maurice and Katia Krafft. This video showed underwater lava as it came out from vents on the sea floor. The lava would first appear as an ordinary rock, next, a luminous fissure or crack would appear across the rock, and then, as the pressure built up inside, the lava would appear to stream out from within the rock. When the lava met the cool ocean water, it would harden into a solid rock again, and repeat the sequence. It had the appearance of an egg hatching. (This is now technically known as "pillow lava.")

R.T. Rundle Clark says, "The egg was invisible, for it took shape before the appearance of light. In fact, *the bird of light burst forth from the egg.*"[18] (my emphasis)

*Volcanic "egg."
Photo courtesy of
NOAA.*

It is entirely possible that an ancient swimmer dove beneath the waters of a lake or sea and observed this process. Somewhat like this, our scientists now observe the volcanic seamount off the southeast coast of the Big Island of Hawaii.

Here are some relevant quotes from the Book of the Dead. Note the volcanic possibilities:

- I am the equipped Ba (soul) who is in this egg of the Addju-fish (form of Horus) I am the Great Cat who is in the Place of Truth in which the light shines forth. [19]
- ... on the day when the sky was choked and stifled, when the Rejected One panted for breath in vivifying Him who was in the Egg ... [20]
- ... it (the Egg) opens with fire, and its breath is destruction to noses and nostrils. [21]
- I keep watch over the Egg ... I grow and flourish [as] it grow and flourish. [22]

Osiris (Asar): God of Geological Forces?

Perhaps this section is superfluous to some. Not blinded by

metaphysical, abstract, spiritual, mystical or extraterrestrial interpretations, it may seem obvious to you that Osiris, the God of the Underworld, was the Volcano God (the God controlling lava, magma, fire-ash flows, mud-flows, lava bombs, etc.).

Although most people have heard of Ra, the Sun God, Osiris was more important. Samuel A. B. Mercer, a noted Egyptian scholar, writes that in the Pyramid Texts, in the earliest hieroglyphs, the name Ra occurs more than 250 times, whereas the name Osiris appears almost 300 times.[23]

E.A. Wallis Budge says of him, "for about four thousand years he remained the great type and symbol of the resurrection ... at no time in Egypt's long history do we find that the position of Osiris was usurped by any other god."[24] Of course, as I mentioned at the beginning of this article, there seems to have been a kind of merging of all Gods into Light-Fire.

Budge notes that the earliest hieroglyphic form of the name "Osiris" was two symbols. A seat or throne and an eye. It may be that the throne refers to a volcano, and the eye to the crater of the volcano. In other words, the smooth surface of the Earth is punctuated by a rising mountain, which could be considered a seat or throne of a God.

Here are some relevant quotes:

- The Two Lands flourish in vindication because of you in the presence of the Lord of All [Ra] ... [Osiris] took possession of the Two Lands even in the womb of Nut [the sky Goddess]; he rules the plains of the Silent Land ...[25]
- May [Osiris] grant power ... to go in and out without hindrance at all the gates of the Duat.[26]

The "Duat" here is the Underworld. The "gates of the Duat" sound to me like volcanic vents or craters leading down into the Underworld. The "Silent Land" may refer to the area beneath the surface of the Earth. This is probably one of the "Two Lands."

It should be noted that the name, "Book of the Dead," is slang. Its real name is the book of "going forth by day" (per em hru). In other words, the book of being reborn. The newly dead person must meet with Osiris. He must undergo the "Weighing of the Heart" ceremony, in which his heart is weighed on a balanced scale against the feather of Maat (truth, justice). Then, the hieroglyphs say,

May he [the dead person] come in freely, may he go out in peace from the House of Osiris, without being expelled or turned back.[27]

In Chapter 147, it talks about the *efflux* (outflow) of Osiris.

The newly dead person says to Osiris,

> I have come before you, the one purified by the efflux within you ...[28]

Also referring perhaps to lava flow is this quote from Chapter 63B,

> I am that equipped oar with which Ra is rowed when the Old Ones are rowed and the efflux [outflow] of Osiris is upraised at the Lake of Flames which does not burn.[29]

The efflux (outflow) of Osiris would be the lava, of course, and the Lake of Flames is probably the lava lake in the volcanic crater, such as existed at Nyiragongo, near the source of the Nile.

According to noted scholar Wallis Budge, the priests at Heliopolis kept a sacred object known as the efflux (outflow) of Osiris in a sealed box. The Coffin Texts, Spell 1080, say:

> This is the sealed thing which is in darkness, with fire about it, which contains the efflux (outflow) of Osiris.

It sounds to me like the priests had collected some lava (which of course then would cool to form volcanic rock).

In Chapter 151, Book of the Dead, we have an interesting combination of Hapy and Osiris:

> I am Hapy, your son, O Osiris Ani [Ani is the newly dead scribe and it is common to connect him with Osiris as much as possible] I have come that I may be your protection and that I may knit together your head and your limbs ... I have given you your head eternally.[30]

Lava, of course, would be a way to "knit together" islands that have been separated by a volcanic explosion. The "head" here may refer to the topmost portion of the volcano. Hapy, usually translated as the God of the Nile, sounds here like liquid lava rather than liquid water.

Here are two additional quotes relevant to Osiris.

- Ho! Fear and Tremble, you Violent Ones who are on the storm-cloud of the Sky! He (Osiris) splits open the earth by means of what he knew when he wished to come thence. Pyramid Texts, Utterance 254.
- ... who were witnesses to resurrection when the corpse of Osiris entered the mountain and the soul of Osiris walked out shining ... when he came forth from death, a shining thing, his face white with heat. Book of the Dead (Ellis translation).

Finally, here is a gem I found in the "Book of the Dead" that undoubtedly refers to a volcanic eruption:

> bring me the ferryboat ... in order to escape from that evil land in which the stars that fall upside down upon their faces and are unable to raise themselves up.[31]

The "stars that fall...and are unable to raise themselves" are probably lava bombs. (See photo at front of book.)

Although this reference was exciting to me, tending to confirm the theory, I had no idea that what I was about to find would amaze me even more, and have repercussions far beyond ancient Egypt.

2 ☼

Volcanic Lightning Bolts

> *Generally speaking, the imagery of Greek mythological descriptions, of battles between Gods and Giants owes something to volcanic phenomena.*
>
> Professor Luce, Dublin University

Before we get to the key finding of this chapter, volcanic lightning, let's examine a few other geological ideas and see how they fit the theory.

Lake of Fire

As I mentioned, the hieroglyphs talk several times of a "Lake of Fire" or "Lake of Flames." From a geological standpoint we have the Virunga Mountains (Smoking Mountains), just west of Lake Victoria near the source of the Nile. There are eight great volcanic cones more than 10,000 feet high: Nyamulagira, Nyiragongo, Mikeno, Karisimbi, Vishoke, Sabinyo, Gahinga and Muhavura (M'fumbiro). Only Nyamulagira and Nyiragongo still are active, and eruptions and lava flows are frequent.

Nyiragongo had a liquid lava pool in its main crater, which was three-fourths of a mile across and 460 meters deep. In 1977, this liquid lake of fire drained out of its base in less than an hour, causing destruction of forests, farms and roads.

Another volcanic lake in the Afar region of East Africa has been active for the last 90 years. It is quite possible that volcanic lakes from this region influenced the Nile River Valley settlers.[32]

Island of Fire

The hieroglyphs also frequently mention an "Island of Fire." For example, from the "Book of the Dead" I found:

O you who bring the ferryboat of Ra, strengthen your rope in the north wind. Ferry upstream to the Island of Fire beside the realm of the dead.[33]

The "realm of the dead" is deep inside the volcano in the Underworld. Here is another quote from the Coffin Texts, Spell 316:

Look with your faces, O God of eld! O Primeval Ancestors!
upon this spirit who comes today, taking the form of a beam of light, coming up from the Isle of Fire. "I have to raise my hand to shad myself, for fear of the fire in her mouth," says one of the elder gods.

What could this be geologically? Lake Turkana is one of the shallow lakes formed as part of the eastern portion of the Great African Rift. There are three volcanic islands in this lake: North Island, Central Island and South Island.

There also have been volcanoes appearing in the Red Sea, which could be the "Island of Fire." Of course, "Island of Fire" could also refer to any of the many volcanoes throughout the world that the Egyptians may have seen or heard about. Read this:

Osiris, the greatest of the gods. I have given unto him the region of the dead. And verily, his son Horus is seated upon the throne of the Dweller in the fiery Lake, as his heir.[34]

Natron Lake

The hieroglyphs refer to a Natron Lake. I found one large Natron Lake (that's its real name) in Tanzania near the famous volcano Kilimanjaro. The lake is the result of geological forces. The Egyptians used natron in their embalming process.

26

Turquoise Lake

The hieroglyphs mention a turquoise (blue-green) lake. This color of lake is frequently seen in the craters of volcanoes. The yellow sulfur from the volcano gives the lakes their greenish color.

Great Lakes

The hieroglyphs mention "great lakes." There are no great lakes in Egypt. These probably refer to the great lakes created by the African rift system, which include Lake Victoria, Lake Albert, Lake Edward, Lake Kivu, Lake Tanganyika and Lake Malawi.

Djed (or Tet) Pillar

I think this column or backbone of Osiris probably was the "volcanic needles" that have been seen at the sites of volcanic eruptions.[35] A volcanic needle occurs when a large chunk of lava is suddenly thrust upward. Here is a quote from the Book of the Dead:

> The Djed column saith: I have come quickly, and I have driven back the footsteps of the god whose face is hidden. I have illuminated his sanctuary. I stand behind the sacred Djed on the Day of Repulsing Disaster. I protect Osiris.[36]

Serpents

Wadjet was the serpent Goddess. The "Book of the Dead," says,

> The goddess Wadjet comes to you in the form of the living Uraeus to anoint your head [the volcano] with her flames. She rises up on the left side of your head and she shines from the right side of your temples without speech; she rises up on your head during each and every hour of the day, even as she does for her father Ra [fire-light], and through her the terror which you inspire in the spirits is increased ... she will never leave you.[37] [my comments]

Here, we again see a reference to lava. There is also a "Primeval Serpent." In fact, throughout the ancient hieroglyphs is frequent mention of serpents. These references pertain to magma, lava flows, earthquakes and ash flows. Even modern volcanologists sometimes describe winding lava flows as serpent-like. Also Ra himself is shown on his hieroglyph surrounded by a serpent.

The many references to serpents (or snakes) were references

to the lava that came out of the ground and then snaked downhill. Also, as a snake can shed its skin and grow new skin, so can a volcano explode and spread itself out over many miles into the atmosphere and then grow a completely new skin or covering.

Living in Southern California for over twenty-five years, I frequently have been jolted by powerful earthquakes and their aftershocks. One cannot help but feel that the land is alive, and that there exists some powerful entity deep within the Earth. It is easy for me to see how ancient humans could have imagined this to be a God, Osiris, or a Primeval Serpent.

The White Crown: Volcanic Sulfur Deposits?

Osiris often is shown wearing a white crown. No one really knows what this white crown represents. One never has been found in any excavation. However, certain pictures of it look curiously like a volcano.

White sulfur compounds surrounding a vent of "child of Krakatau." Photo by author.

In 1997, on the child of Krakatau in the Sunda Strait, our party explored many volcanic openings or vents, technically called "fumaroles." The vents often give off sulfur gases and surrounding these vents, as well as parts of the main crater, is a mostly white, powdery substance that is sulfur, as well as sulfuric acids combined with minerals. (Although sulfur is usually yellowish, the sulfate minerals known as anhydrides give this powder its very white color.)

From a boat, white sulfur compounds are visible on "child of Krakatau." Photo by author.

The white deposits, sitting around the tops of vents and the crater, look to an observer like a white crown. I believe that the sulfur deposits led to the beginning of alchemy, which later became chemistry. Early humans may have investigated this white substance and developed knowledge of its uses. In support of this, "The Book of the

Dead" says,

> I am the possessor of the Wereret-crown [White Crown], the assistant of the magicians.

An early alchemist probably would be considered a magician, and sulfur is considered "one of the four basic raw materials of the chemical industry." In fact, sulfur is one of the basic ingredients of black powder (later called gun powder). Magicians, even today, frequently are associated with some type of fire-powder or flash-powder.

Volcanic Lightning . . . A Key to Ancient Mythology

It was with much delight that I discovered Mott C. Greene's book, *Natural Knowledge in Preclassical Antiquity*. Mott Greene is a professor at the University of Puget Sound in Seattle, and a MacArthur Fellow. In his book, he suggests that certain important passages in classical Greek texts are linked with certain volcanic eruptions in the Mediterranean.

Specifically, Greene discusses Hesiod (8th century BC), a famous Greek author who wrote a work called *Theogony* (the origin of the Gods). In this book, there is an important battle between Zeus and the Titans, which is called the Titanomachy. The Titans had ruled the cosmos, but after this battle, Zeus and his allies ruled. Greene shows rather convincingly that this battle was the huge eruption of the volcano (Santorini) on the island of Thera around 1628 BC.

Greene notes an important point: "the arrival of Zeus at the climactic moment."[38] Zeus, if you remember, has the weapon of lightning (and its resulting air shock wave called thunder.) In the European and US cultures, we equate lightning with thunderstorms, like the ones that I saw rolling across the plains of North America when I was a child. I had no idea that lightning also could be linked to volcanoes.

Even the general populace, being somewhat familiar with volcanoes from television documentaries, does not tend to think of lightning linked to a volcano. Thus, it was quite a revelation to me to see the video "Ring Of Fire: East Of Krakatoa (1998)." Two brothers who spent 10 years traveling through Indonesia made the video, part of a series, "Ring of Fire." In the video, (on Google Videos now) we see Krakatau, in the middle of the Sunda Strait, *with a clear, blue sky overhead.* Yet, as the volcanic ash and smoke rise from the crater, we see lightning flashing down into the crater of the volcano. (You can now find many videos of volcanic lightning on the Internet.)

When I first saw this I was electrified, for it was the first time I had ever thought of Zeus linked to a volcano rather than a thunderstorm. It seemed to fit nicely with my overall theory.

I cannot emphasize the importance of this volcanic lightning enough. Even though I have seen this phenomenon on videotape, my Midwestern American upbringing still wants me to link Zeus with traditional, non-volcanic thunderstorms! So, it may take some major reconditioning (unless you live near a volcano) before you are able to understand what I am talking about.

The volcano-lightning phenomenon is discussed in some detail in an important article appearing in the journal *Science,* in 1965, entitled, "Electricity in Volcanic Clouds." European and US scientists studied this volcanic lightning in the volcano island, Surtsey, which first rose above the ocean near Iceland in 1963. I have since investigated a number of volcanoes and have found that volcanic lightning occurs frequently during eruptions. For example, volcanic lightning has been observed at the eruptions of Krakatau (1883), Vesuvius (1906), Heimaey (1973), Mount St. Helens (1980), Redoubt (1990) and at other volcanoes.[39]

Apparently, as the ash and gas are ejected into the sky by the volcano, a positive electrical energy charge is formed due to friction with the air, much as when you rub your socks across a rug. The lightning then *dis*charges this energy (like when you touch a doorknob).[40]

Greene says that gives the appearance of "lightning bolts being hurled into the mouth of the crater across a distance of several kilometers."[41] Again, remember the sky is blue and there are no clouds except the rising ash cloud from the volcano.

Ancient Misinterpretation

In the table below, Greene shows the correspondence as the events progress.[42] Greene states:

In other words, at the climatic breach of the integrity of the magma chamber at Thera, huge volleys of volcanic lightning immediately preceded the final phreatomagmatic collapse of the caldera with its associated heat and noise — and the end of the Titans, giving rise to the interpretation (in Hesiod) that Zeus's intervention was decisive. The volcano exhausts itself and disappears beneath the ocean, the Titans are bound beneath the earth: end of the Titanomachy and arrival of the hegemony of Zeus.[43]

A long war has already been fought between the Olympiads and the Titans before this engagement.	premonitory seismicity
Both sides gather strength for a final encounter; Zeus's allies, the "hundred-handers," grasp massive rocks.	increase activity
There are terrible echoes from over the sea.	first phase explosions
The ground rumbles loudly.	tectonic earthquakes
The sky shakes and groans.	air shock waves
Mount Olympus trembles all over at the moment of contact of the opponents.	great earthquakes
There are steady vibrations of the ground — like the stamping of innumerable feet running.	earthquakes
Weapons whistle through the air.	pyroclastic ejecta, massive rocks thrown
Loud battle cries are shouted, reaching up to the high heavens.	explosive reports
Advent of thunder and lightning signal the arrival of Zeus — a solid roll of sacred fire. Fertile fields crackle and burn. Forests roar with fire.	volcanic lightning, heat of fine-grained volcanic rocks
Earth and ocean streams and barren sea begin to boil.	magma chamber breach
An immense flame shoots up into the air, enveloping the Titans in a blast of hot air, apparently as a blindingly bright flash, and as prodigious heat.	phreatomagmatic explosion
The sight and sound are so enormous that one would think the sky had collapsed onto the Earth and smashed it.	sound of above
Arrival of wind-born dust with lightning and thunder, with a deafening uproar.	final ash eruptions
Titans are buried under a cloud of missiles and bound beneath the Earth.	collapsed debris

Today, we have workable models of friction, electricity and lightning, and we describe the events from the standpoint of those models. We know the volcanic eruption *causes* the lightning.

Ancient humans saw the volcanic lightning as an independent event (Zeus) rather than caused by the eruptive particles. They thought that the inevitable collapse of the volcano (the defeat of the Titans), due to the emptying of the magma chamber, was caused by the volcanic lightening (Zeus). To them, it appears that Zeus had won the battle.

Thus, ancient humans misinterpreted causation. Greene's astute analysis of the final events gave me a key I needed to understand an important element of the ancient Egyptian texts.

Battle I: Osiris Versus Seth

Hieroglyphs (or their translations) can be a confusing array. However, Egyptologists agree that they refer to two main battles in their past.

31

The first was what I call, "Osiris versus Seth."

Nile River Hieroglyphs	Combatants	Winner
Battle I	Osiris vs. Seth	Seth
Battle II	Horus vs. Seth	Horus

In this battle, one of the most ancient after the rise of the Primeval Mount from the Primeval Waters, we have a battle between Osiris and Seth. In the geological interpretation, Osiris would represent the volcano and Seth the volcanic lightning. In this battle, Seth wins and Osiris is blown to bits and scattered. Mercer calls this event "one of the most central and important elements in ancient Egyptian thought."[44] Budge notes one erroneous version of this event by Plutarch (that has been widely quoted), in which Osiris is tricked into lying in a box and later cut into pieces.[45] However, even this version agrees with the mutilation of Osiris.

Seth is usually referred to as the God of Storms. The "Book of the Dead," says:

...for I am Seth, who sets up the storms and thunder within the horizon of the sky, like a fury.[46]

Of course, in this aspect he resembles Zeus. Thanks to help from Mott Greene, we can see that the Osiris-Seth battle was similar to the Titan-Zeus battle. In both cases, the God of Storms (Seth or Zeus) is the victor over the volcanic forces (Osiris or Titans).

I suggest that this event was an ancient eruption of a volcano in a sea or a lake, possibly similar to the 1883 Krakatau explosion or ancient Thera explosions. The "Book of the Dead" may even mention the parts of Osiris that were blown away. Chapter 18:

...it was when there was the burial of the forearms, the flanks, and the thighs of Osiris.[47]

Thus, it appears that the entire *midsection* of Osiris was destroyed. If one looks at a diagram of Krakatau before the 1883 eruption it has a curious similarity to the V-shape of a man's body. Remarkably, similar to the Osiris legend, it was mostly the midsection of this "body" that was blown away in 1883. (However, other hieroglyphs mention other body parts.)

I am not saying that the specific volcano was Krakatau. It may have been Thera or another or both. For it appears that like

Krakatau, Thera also erupts periodically. Evidence indicates that in the last 200,000 years it has had "at least 12 large eruption explosions."[48]

Just as in the case of the child of Krakatau, a child of Osiris appears. His name is Horus. His sister, Isis, nurtures him in secret. If we look at a diagram of Krakatau after 1883, we see two islands to the left and right of the empty center, where the "child of Krakatau" will grow. These are similar to the sisters of Osiris, Isis and Nephthys. In fact, Osiris is sometimes represented between Isis and Nephthys. Perhaps Isis and Nephthys represent the islands surrounding the central newborn volcano.

Osiris between Isis and Nephthys' wings, from the Book of the Dead.)

Important to this event, and our geological interpretation of it, is Chapter 108 of "The Book of the Dead." It appears this chapter of the Book of the Dead may be an accurate description of an ancient volcanic explosion. Here is the first part of it: [My comment and my emphasis in brackets.]

As for that mountain of Bakhu on which the sky rests, it is in the east of the sky; it is three hundred rods long and one hundred and fifty rods broad. Sobk, Lord of Bakhu, is in the east of that mountain; his temple is of carnelian [a *reddish* variety of quartz]. A serpent is on the top of that mountain; it is thirty cubits long, eight cubits of its forepaws are of *flint*, and its teeth *gleam*. I know the name of this *serpent* which is on the mountain; its name is, *'he who is in his burning.'*[49]

I think this serpent on the mountain is the lava in the volcanic crater. Its temple is "red" like lava, forepaws are like flint (which is a spark-producing and thus fire-producing rock), it's teeth "gleam" like lava, and its name is "he who is in his burning." The glyphs go on with a key part: [My comments.]

Now after awhile he [the serpent] will turn his eyes against Ra, and a stoppage will occur in the Sacred Bark [the boat that carries Ra, or disk of the sun] and a great vision among the crew [the other gods with Ra], for he will swallow up seven cubits of the great waters; Seth will project a lance of iron against him and will make him vomit up all that he has swallowed. [50]

Geologists still debate the exact manner in which Krakatau exploded in 1883.[51] However, one widely accepted hypothesis is the "collapse hypothesis." In this hypothesis, the emptying of the magma chamber causes the collapse of the island, the seawater rushes in, contacts the magma, and is vaporized in what is called a "phreatomagmatic" explosion (phreatic = ground water + magma). Greene describes this as like the "explosion of a giant steam boiler."[52] Rupert Furneaux, in the 1964 book *Krakatau*, presents this reconstructed scenario of the 1883 eruption:

> At ten o'clock plus two minutes, three-quarters of Krakatau Island ... collapsed into the chasm beneath. Nineteen hours of continuous eruption had drained the magma from the chamber faster than it could be replenished from below. Krakatau's three cones caved in. The sea bed reared and opened in upheaval. The sea rushed into the gaping hole. From the raging cauldron of seething rocks, frothing magma and hissing sea spewed an immense quantity of water. Up from the volcano shot huge rocks. A cloud of dust and debris rose high in the sky ... It was blacker than the blackest night. [Also later in the text:] Sky streaked with lightning.

If we compare Furneaux's description with that from the "Book of the Dead," we see a remarkable similarity. (The "stoppage" of the Sacred Bark probably was the blocking out of the Sun.) The only thing that Furneaux has failed to mention is the volcanic lightning, which he mentions later in his text as "Sky streaked with lightning."[53]

So, we see a one-to-one correspondence between the two events:

Book of the Dead Report	Volcanic Eruption Report
The serpent swallows up seven cubits of the great water.	The sea rushed into the gaping hole.
Seth will project a lance or iron at him.	Sky streaked with lightning.
Seth will make him vomit up all he has swallowed.	Spewing an immense quantity of water; up from the volcano shot huge rocks.
a stoppage will occur in the Sacred Bark (the solar boat of Ra).	It was blacker than the blackest night.

Note that, "a stoppage will occur in the Sacred Bark" is the type of wording frequently used to justify appealing to cataclysmic events such as a comet or asteroid impacting the Earth. However, it is doubtful to me that even a large impact, within humankind's memory, would have enough force to cause the Earth to temporarily stop rotating and thus give the appearance of the Sun stopping in the sky.

This is not to say that past cosmic collisions have not occurred. In fact, we know they have occurred as we have detected the scars on the Earth. These collisions may trigger volcanic eruptions.

However, after the dinosaur extinction comet was proposed, cosmic collisions became a fashion for explaining mythology. While there may be some myths that refer to ancient collisions with asteroids or comets, a brief flash across the sky followed by darkness, fires, floods, etc., does not allow close scrutiny over long periods of time like a volcano does. A volcano inspires creation stories. A volcano makes one think of God. Just visit one and you will see (but don't get too close).

Battle II: Horus Versus Seth

For Battle II, Horus versus Seth, noted Egyptologist R. T. Rundle Clark gives his summary:[54]

- Horus and Seth fought for supremacy.
- The adventures of the Eye of Horus and the testicles of Seth.
- Thoth persuaded the two contestants to take their dispute to the Council of Gods.
- Horus was awarded supremacy and crowned king.
- Seth became the God of Storms and was put into the boat of the Sun God.
- Horus (or his representative) went down into the underworld to see Osiris.
- Osiris was given the Eye or the good news that Horus was king.
- The soul of Osiris was liberated.
- The reign of Horus.

Instead of one huge, cataclysmic event, it lasts some 80 years.[55] We have the new volcano appearing above the surface of the water and appearing to ancient humans to be engaged in a battle against the God of Storms.

One is again reminded of the child of Krakatau appearing above the waters in 1927. As it erupts and grows, one can intermittently see the volcanic lightning or the "battle" between the God of Storms and the God of the Volcano.

It should be mentioned that the "Eye" is seen frequently in hieroglyphs. It, like the "mouth" or "head," probably is a representation of the crater of the volcano. In the "Coffin Texts" we find Thoth saying this:

> I came seeking the eye of Horus, that I might bring it back and count it. I found it complete, counted and sound, so that it can flame up to the sky and blow above and below.[56]

This "flame" sounds to me remarkably like a volcanic eruption.

At one point of this second battle, Seth destroys the Eye of Horus for a time. In Chapter 112 of the "Book of the Dead," Budge notes that Seth transformed himself into a black pig:

> Horus looked at the black pig into which Seth had transformed himself, and at once received a terrible blow of fire in the eye, and through the whirlwind of fire which followed it the eye was destroyed.[57]

The "black pig" of course would be the black cloud of the volcanic eruption. The "blow of fire" was the crashing of a huge lightning volley into the crater, or eye, at the same time that the crater collapsed and was blown to smithereens in the *phreatomagmatic* explosion that followed.

Later, the Eye of Horus is restored just as we would expect of an active and growing volcano. Chapter 17 of the "Book of the Dead" describes it:

> The combat that took place on the day when Horus fought with Seth, during which Seth threw filth in the face of Horus, and Horus crushed the genitals of Seth. The filling of the utchat [the restoration of the light to the eye of Horus] Thoth performed with his own fingers. I remove the thunder cloud from the sky when there is a storm with thunder and lightning therein. What is this? This storm was the raging of Ra at the thunder-cloud which [Seth] sent forth against the right eye of Ra. [comments are Budge's][58]

We again see the thunder and lightning, which easily could be the volcanic phenomenon we have discussed. My interpretation is that ancient humans thought that Seth caused the black clouds of ash and dust that rose out of the volcano, accompanied by volcanic lightning. They felt that Ra disliked this black cloud, as during a major eruption it would block out the Sun (Ra) for days.

It is possible that the crushing of the "genitals of Seth" refers to the fact that genitals in a male are responsible for the deep voice. This deep voice may have been the thunder associated with Seth.

When Seth is defeated then, in effect, his genitals are crushed.

Finally, Horus and Seth are brought before the council of Gods, and Thoth (the God of learning, writing and knowledge) intervenes on behalf of Horus. I think the volcano entered a period of dormancy.

The Resurrection of Osiris: The Growth of the Volcano?

As Clark mentions, Osiris is given the Eye of Horus. We have Osiris being, in essence, resurrected as Horus. Budge says, "Horus first came to Osiris, who was in the state of a dead man, and embraced him. By this embrace he transferred to him either his own Ka (double) or a portion of the power which dwelt in it."[59] Later, "when Osiris received it [the eye of Horus], he received into himself a soul, that is a new life, or revivification ... Osiris was made to live a second time."[60]

In Budge's book, *Osiris and the Egyptian Resurrection*, we have the following passages from the ancient hieroglyphs of Teta (Teta here is the newly dead person who is linked to Osiris):

Hail, thou Osiris Teta, stand up! Horus cometh ... Horus loveth thee. He hath filled thee with his Eye, he has joined his Eye to thee ... He hath given thee his Eye which flourisheth lastingly. He hath given thee thy weapon, thou has conquered all thine enemies. Horus has filled thee wholly with his eye ...[61]

It is easy for me to imagine a volcanic interpretation here. Horus, the new volcano, has his "Eye," the active flaming crater, which possibly was believed by the ancient humans to be now connected to Osiris, who represented the God of the volcanic forces and magma beneath the Earth.

The "Book of the Dead," Chapter 183 (Faulkner translation) says:

[Atum or Ra] has stopped the raging tumult for you [Osiris], and the Two Lands are peacefully reconciled before you ... The throne of Geb has been allotted to him [Horus] ... The kingship of Geb has been given to you [Horus], for he is your father who created your beauty ... You [Osiris] have appeared as lord of the Two Lands ... Life is with you, food follows after you ...[62]

We see here what may be more references to volcanoes and the fertile soil that comes from them.

Of course, as Budge suggests, the Osiris resurrection may have later influenced resurrection in Christianity.

The Flood: Volcanic Tidal Wave?

The flood that is mentioned in the Book of the Dead usually is thought to be the yearly flooding of the Nile. However, nowhere in the Book of the Dead is the word "yearly" mentioned, or the word "annual," or any other similar word. As geologist Dorothy Vitaliano says, "the annual flood could never have been anything but benign on the whole. Its failure to materialize would have been the disaster to commemorate in legend."[63]

There are many references to some sort of catastrophic event. Chapter 18 specifically discusses this event. Dr. Goelet merely states that part of this chapter refers to "an event or ritual in the mythological past."[64] However, let us see if it makes more sense from a geological viewpoint. Look at these passages from that chapter:[65] [My comment in brackets.]

- on that night of the Evening Meal, on that night of battle, at the moment of guarding of the rebels [Seth and his allies], and on that day of destroying the enemies of the Lord of All [Ra].
- as to 'that night of the Evening Meal,' it is dawn at the burial of Osiris.
- on that night of Isis spending the night awake, mourning over her brother Osiris.
- which is in Abydos [ancient town sacred to Osiris] on that night of the Haker-festival [festival celebrating the death and birth of Osiris] when the dead are counted and the Blessed Spirits are chosen ...
- the council who judge the dead on that night of making an accounting of their dead.
- the hacking up of the earth of Busiris [city sacred to Osiris] on that night of hacking the earth with their blood and vindicating Osiris against his enemies.
- in the presence of the Great Council [council of Gods] ... on that night of secreting of forms.
- As to 'that night of secreting of forms': it was when there was the burial of the forearm, the flanks and the thighs of Osiris.

The references to a "battle," the "hacking up of the earth," the "burial" of Osiris, the "accounting of their dead," the "secreting of forms," make one think of a volcanic explosion. My interpretation is that this event of Chapter 18 was an ancient explosion of a volcano. Possibly, it was a volcanic island of Lake Turkana, or the volcano Santorini (on Thera), or Krakatau, or another.

Here is a reference to a flood from part of Chapter 175 of the

38

"Book of the Dead." Ani, the recently dead scribe, asks Atum, the red Sun-God at its setting, how long he will live. Atum answers:

> You shall be for millions on millions of years. I will dispatch the Elders [the ancient Gods of the volcano?] and destroy all that I have made; the earth shall return to the Primordial Water, to the surging flood, as in its original state. But I will remain with Osiris, I will transform myself into something else, namely a serpent, without men ever knowing or the gods seeing ... I have given him [Osiris] the desert, and his son Horus is the heir on the throne which is in the Island of Fire. [66] [my comments]

Here we see the ancient fire-light as represented by Atum transforming into a serpent under the Earth.

The Unification of the Two Lands

The Unification of the Two Lands may not refer to political unification of North and South Egypt, as is traditionally thought, and at least one Egyptologist, Jane Sellers, agrees with me on this. Although she thinks it refers to astronomical phenomena, I think a geological interpretation is much more likely. Here is a relevant passage from the Memphite Theology. Geb is the God of the Earth:

> [Geb, lord of the gods, commanded] that the Nine Gods gather to him. He judged between Horus and Seth; he ended their quarrel. He made Seth king of Upper Egypt in the land of Upper Egypt, up to the place in which he was born, which is Su. And Geb made Horus king of Lower Egypt in the land of Lower Egypt, up to the place in which his father was drowned which is "Division-of-the-Two-Lands." Thus Horus stood over one region, and Seth stood over one region. They made peace over the Two Lands at Ayan. That was the division of the Two Lands.
> Geb's words to Seth: "Go to the place in which you were born." Seth: Upper Egypt. Geb's words to Horus: "Go to the place in which your father was drowned." Horus: Lower Egypt. Geb's words to Horus and Seth: "I have separated you." — Lower and Upper Egypt. [67]

In other words, I think that the "Two Lands" may refer to 1) the "land" above ground that Seth "stood over," and 2) the land below ground that Horus "stood over." Geb, as the God of the Earth, separates Seth, of the atmosphere, and Horus, of the magma.

We will see this type of separation metaphor in later cultures.

Isis

The traditional myth says that Isis nurtured Horus in secret. This fits with Isis being the remnants of the volcano Osiris. Osiris emerged from the primeval ocean (or great lake) and was blown to bits. Under the water, the new volcano, Horus, slowly grew, as did the child of Krakatau from 1883 until 1927 when it emerged from the ocean.

Phoenix (Bennu-Bird)

The seagoing Phoenicians took their name from the mythical bird, the Phoenix. (In ancient Egypt, the Phoenix was referred to as the Bennu-bird.) One Phoenix lived at any one time and it lived for a very long time. The Encyclopedia Britannica says, "No ancient authority gives it a life span of less than 500 years; some say it lives for 1461 years (an Egyptian Sothic Period): an extreme estimate is 97,200 years." A purple-red color, the bird was said, "to burn itself on a funeral pyre and to rise from its ashes in the freshness of youth and live through another cycle of years."[68] Its miraculous rebirth and its connection with fire have led scholars to associate it with the Sun. However, volcanoes, like this Phoenix, have periods of dormancy and rebirth. The purple-red color is the colors I saw when trekking over the lava in Hawaii and Indonesia. The dried lava is purple. The red is the lava before it cools. The regeneration fits with the theme of a volcano rising from its ashes. The Phoenix was very likely not the Sun, but a volcano.

Ankh

The ankh (see drawing by author) is commonly thought to represent a sandal by many scholars. Let us examine it from the "volcanic perspective" and see if it makes more sense. Here is some information on the Ankh:

The Ankh is defined as: The symbolic representation of both Physical and Eternal life. It is known as the original cross ... It is also a symbol for the power to give and sustain life. The Ankh is typically associated with material things such as water (which was believed by Egyptians to regenerate life), air, sun, as well as with the Gods, who are frequently pictured carrying an Ankh. The Egyptian king is often associated with the Ankh also, either in possession of an Ankh (providing life to

his people) or being given an Ankh (or stream of Ankhs) by the Gods ... It is usually worn as an amulet to extend the life of the living and placed on the mummy to energize the resurrected spirit. The Gods and the Kings are often shown carrying the Ankh to distinguish them from mere mortals. The Ankh symbolized eternal life and bestowed immortality on anyone who possessed it...The amulet is a powerful talisman that provides the wearer with protection from the evil forces of decay and degeneration. The loop of the Ankh is held by the Gods. It is associated with Isis and Osiris in the Early Dynastic Period...It is usually held to the nose of the deceased king by the Gods to represent the breath of life given in the after-world. The Ankh also resembles a key and is considered the key to eternal life after death. Its influence was felt in every dynastic period and survives as an icon possessing mystical power throughout the Coptic Christian era. The Ankh possessed by each God had power associated with that God.[69]

Thus, the ankh can be easily interpreted as representing a volcano. The bottom vertical part representing the magma underneath the Earth, the horizontal section representing the surface of the Earth where the magma hardened into lava and thereby allowed life. The upper loop could represent either: a) the upper part of the volcano, b) the atmospheric outgassing, or c) the apparent loop of the Sun across the sky.

The ankh unifies Upper and Lower Egypt, the magma below and the Earth, the sky and the Sun above. It is part of the Grand Unification Theory of the ancients.

Summary

Alan Alford's book, *The Phoenix Solution*, interprets the ancient Egyptian religion as describing an exploding planet between Mars and Jupiter. He was right in one respect: there was an exploding planet, but it was not another planet, it was ours.

I did not have to dig deep to find all these volcanic references. In fact, looking at the "Pyramid Texts," the "Coffin Texts," the "Book of the Dead," and other references, I am overwhelmed by the number of what seem to be geological or volcanic references.

The chart on the next page summarizes the findings I have discussed in the last two chapters.

Ancient Egypt	Traditional Meaning	Geological Meaning
Atum	Ra at "sunset" (reddish Sun goes to underworld to be recharged by red magma)	atmospheric particles bend light to make reddish color; Earth spins away from its home star.
Primeval Mound/Primeval Waters	creation myth	volcanic island
Phallus of Ra	unknown	A volcano & its lava outflow
Cosmic Egg	creation myth	Underwater lava flow (looks like egg hatching) forms pillow basalts
Osiris	God of the Underworld	geological forces, volcanoes, earthquakes
throne of Geb (Earth)	unknown	mountain or volcano
efflux (outflow) of Osiris	unknown	lava flow
Duat, Netherworld, Silent Land	living place of Osiris	magma beneath the earth
Lake of Fire	place connected with the underworld	lava lake (possibly Nyiragongo)
Isle of Fire	place connected with the underworld	volcanic island in a sea or lake (Lake Turkana?)
Turquoise Lakes	Unknown	volcanic lakes that sulfur turns blue-green
Djed or (tet) pillar	backbone of Osiris	volcanic needles
Serpents	mythical monsters	magma, lava flows
White Crown of Osiris	Symbolic of Upper Egypt	white sulfur compounds at volcanic vents
Red Crown of Osiris	Symbol of Lower Egypt	magma beneath volcano
Seth (or Set)	God of chaos, storms	volcanic lightning
Horus	Son of Osiris	reappearance of volcano after explosion from under the sea or lake
The Unification of the Two Lands	political unification of South and North Egypt	both underworld and sky unified after eruption as crust
Isis	wife-sister of Osiris, mother of Horus	outer, ring-shaped remnants of volcanic-island explosion
Pyramids	place to transform pharaoh into Osiris	represents volcanoes and biosphere recycling
Sphinx	unknown (rebirth of pharaoh as lion-god?)	hardened lava takes strange shapes like lion

Conclusions

I am aware that what I am proposing here is a major paradigm shift from:

A) the Nile River civilization developing solely from local sources, in which early man was concerned with magical and seemingly incomprehensible chants (mumbo jumbo) to guide the dead person by way of mysterious stone monuments into an abstract heaven with abstract Gods, to,

B) the Nile River civilization traveling to or being influenced by peoples or legends from the volcanoes/geology of the Great Rift Valley and/or other geologically active areas, in which early man was concerned with the guiding of the dead person, via a pyramid structure, which mimicked a volcano, into a "rebirth" as new lava, with Gods that represented real things such as volcanoes, lava, volcanic lightning and the Sun.

Undoubtedly, the stars also had their influence on the Nile River Valley people. Through certain alignments in their buildings and pyramids, and in their writings, they recognized these heavenly bodies. I have chosen not to emphasize them because I feel that the geological influences on their thought have been largely, if not completely, ignored.

So why did someone not make the connection between geology and the ancient Nile River Valley civilization before this? Three reasons:

1) The hieroglyphs were translated in the early part of the 1800s. They became firmly established. If you read a book about the ancient Egyptian religion published in the 1800s or early 1900s, it differs very little from a book written today. Meanwhile, the science of volcanology did not get started until after the eruption of Mt. Pelée in 1902 in Martinique.

2) Egyptologists and geologists both face a very competitive job market. They have little time to examine anything outside their fields.

3) Modern Egypt makes billions of dollars yearly on their tourist industry. They are naturally very reluctant to embrace anything new that might upset this income. They also are reluctant to embrace natural explanations, but instead encourage mystery.

It was never necessary for us to believe outlandish theories such as aliens coming from another star system or even exploding planets. Or for us to gather data on Egypt by going into a trance, "channeling," remembering "past lives," or searching for a mysterious "Hall of Records" (as described by Edgar Cayce). What was needed was simply a multidisciplinary approach.

To understand the source of Nile River mythology we needed to go to the source of the Nile River. We needed to go to the African Rift Valley, one of the greatest natural features on the face of this planet. Without this rift system the Nile River would not exist. The

43

uplifting caused by the geological forces created the mountains. When the moist air rises over these mountains, we get condensation and rain. This rain feeds the rivers and lakes, which flow together and slowly work their way down the longest river in the world.

The volcanoes at the source of the Nile River system, and/or other volcanoes, were remembered by being carved into stone symbolized by the huge pyramids (fire-in-the-middle) of Giza, and the volcanic recycling that occurs was imitated by the mummified Pharaohs who wait "to come forth by day" (per em hru), from the magma, in whatever shape they wish. Perhaps they chose to come forth as the Sphinx, with the body of a lion and the head of a man. The Pharaoh-Sphinx today looks eastward, toward the new Sun, the birth of the day.

The mummified Pharaohs wait for their Ba ("soul") to come to reanimate them. They wait for their Ka ("spirit") to reanimate them. However, slowly their atoms disintegrate into the surroundings, despite the best efforts of the ancient embalmers and modern scientists. The atoms become again part of the living, circulating mass of the Earth's biosphere. The Pharaohs have slowed down Mother Nature, but not beaten her. Perhaps someday, if Aubrey de Grey's suggestions in *Ending Aging* are followed, the human dream of immortality will be realized.

Finding volcanoes and geology to be so important in the mythology of ancient Egypt, I predicted that I would also find geological references in other mythological writings throughout the world. I first looked at the Bible, I was completely stunned at what I found.

3 ☼

The Bible's Volcanoes

> *...and Jehovah gave thunder and hail, and the fire would run down to the earth, and Jehovah kept making it rain down hail upon the land of Egypt. Thus there came hail, and fire quivering in among the hail.*
>
> *Exodus 9:22-23*

Judeo-Christian-Islamic Texts: Jehovah and Java

In just the last 10,000 years, there have been 11 active volcanoes in Turkey, three in Iran, 28 in Syria and in Arabia.[70] This count doesn't include the highly active volcanic area of the East African Rift Valley near present day Ethiopia, Eritrea, Djibouti and the Red Sea. However, as I have mentioned, early knowledge of volcanoes may have also spread from other areas. So the people of the Middle East had plenty of volcanic material to observe.

Angels

In this section, I'll present evidence suggesting "angels" are what geologists call lava bombs. A lava bomb is a piece of lava, small or large, that is thrown out of the volcano and flies through the air to land on the side of the volcano. The word "angelos" comes from a word meaning "messenger."

At the front of the book is a photo I took of a drawing on the island of Bali of a primitive angel (the supreme God of this volcanic island) before the flying fiery lava had been transformed into a shining halo and wings. Bright red flames encase the God as he falls to Earth. This image was the first clue for me that angels might be what geologists call lava bombs.

Small lava bomb. Precursor of the "angel." Photo by author.

The word "angelos" also is related to "urn," so we see a possible connection with cinder urns and burning. There is a folk legend in which children are given a cold cinder in their hands to protect them at night (much like an angel would). Thus, these lava bombs or angels at one time were "messengers" from the pit of magma, the abode of Osiris and other Gods.

Satan, the chief angel closest to God, was cast down into the pit of fire. Originally, Satan probably was a volcanic mountain. This would put him "closest to God," at least the God of fire, life, death and resurrection under the crust.

As we read through Malcolm Godwin's book *Angles,* we note the strong resemblance of the medieval ideas of heaven and hell and angels to volcanic activity. It is as if travelers made the trip to see the various volcanoes of the Mediterranean,[71] or had visited other volcanoes and were describing them. He describes Lucifer-Satan: "Bearer of Light ... Dragon of Dawn ... Prince of the Power of Air ... the first to separate himself from the Divine source." "He shares with the serpent the ability to shed the old dead skin and arise as if newborn." (Like the volcanic resurrection of the Phoenix, Krakatau and Thera, which explode and thereby shed their skin, etc.)

Angels are said to be in three Triads (three groups of three). The first triad consisting of the Seraphim, the Cherubim and the Thrones. All of these triads probably are different classifications of lava and embers and ash, in an intricate semantic orchestration.

Godwin says:

Entities radiate outward from His Presence, some being close to the center while others more further and further away from the Divine source of Light and Love ... The highest Triad is made up of the Seraphim, the Cherubim and the Thrones. These are in direct communion with the Divine Unity and receive God's unfiltered Illumination. The next Triad orbiting God is composed of the Dominations, Virtues and Powers who receive Divine Illumination from the first Triad and then in turn transmit it to the lowest triad — the Principalities, Archangels and Angels. These then convey it to us mortal humans ... Thought slows down as it moves from the center and becomes Light, which in turn decelerates to become Heat which condenses into matter.[72]

This is a good early description of a volcano. The Thrones are said to be a point at which matter first appears. This was the lava hardening to rock. God is said to be at the center of a central core and at the highest point. Entities radiate outward from His Presence, away from the Divine Illumination.

In Revelation 20:1 we have

And I saw an angel coming down out of heaven, having the key to the Abyss and holding in his hand a great chain. He seized the dragon, that ancient serpent, who is the devil, or Satan, and bound him for a thousand years. He threw him into the Abyss, and locked and sealed it over him, to keep him from deceiving the nations anymore until the thousand years were ended. After that, he must be set free for a short time.

Being "bound" probably refers to the volcano not erupting. We see again Satan as the volcano. The passage goes on to talk of the devil being thrown into the "lake of burning sulfur." Then the dead are judged to be either resurrected or thrown into "the lake of fire." This, of course, is the same as the Egyptian story and is a primitive attempt to understand the Earth's natural processes and to assign a fit moral ending.

The *Koran* mentions two Archangels: Michael and Gabriel or Micha-el and Gabri-el. The word "el" comes from the Sumerian and means "brightness" or "shining." They also are mentioned in the Old Testament.

When humans were supposedly kicked out of the Garden of Eden (possibly the island of Java), perhaps they had to sweat to cultivate the land. The eruption-explosion of the volcano Krakatau may have forced them to move onto the Sunda Plain or elsewhere, where they learned to domesticate wild rice and barley or other crops. Alternatively, perhaps they moved to areas where volcanoes were scarce and wild fruits were easily available.

Thus, it appears that our legends of glowing angels and the glowing halo are attempts to preserve memories of the fiery rocks, lava bombs that "fly" out of the volcano: "angelos" or messengers from God.

Genesis

"Genesis" means the origin, the creation, or the source. Is it possible that *Genesis* of the Bible is the same creation story as is told in all the other myths of the world? I think so.

The seven days of creation in this story may stem from early humans witnessing a volcano rising somewhat rapidly from the sea. Then they saw how quickly the barren lava turned into fertile soil. Then they saw the appearance of trees, plants birds and eventually humans. They thought this was the way things came into being and they recorded it in their "sacred" stories.

The story of Noah probably was considered sacred because it was an attempt to keep this knowledge alive to prevent a similar devastation from occurring in the future. A similar destruction story also appears in the Egyptian hieroglyphs.

Exodus

You may have heard of the idea that the Exodus of the Egyptians was influenced by the volcanic eruption of Thera in about 1628 BCE (Before the Common Era). Two prominent volcanologists summarize the theory.[73]

- In Exodus, the "darkness which may be felt" could have been caused by falling ash;
- the "waters ... turned to blood," by the wealth of rust-red iron oxide in the volcanic dust which fell into the rivers;
- the "thunder," by the flashes of static electricity produced by friction among the ash [volcanic lightning]; the hail by the crystallization of ice around the volcanic particles;
- the "frogs" by the tornadoes following upon the eruption which, as they passed over lakes, sucked up frogs along with the water;
- the "death of the first-born" and the "ulcers" (boils), by the famine which followed upon the destruction of the harvest and the pollution of the water after the volcanic ash had fallen upon them;
- the proliferation of flies and the pestilence visited upon livestock may be connected with the rotting corpses of animals which had died of starvation;
- lice and locusts may be said to have taken advantage of the destruction of the frogs, fish and birds killed by polluted water, which had habitually preyed upon them.

Judgment Day

Judgment Day was undoubtedly a volcanic explosion or some other violent geological act. Many volcanoes erupt repeatedly. Whether the Judgment Day story stems from Krakatau, Thera or an undersea earthquake, such as the one that killed over 200,000 in 2004, is not clear at present.
In Isaiah 27:1 we read,

In that day,
the LORD will punish with his sword,
his fierce, great and powerful sword,
Leviathan the gliding serpent,
Leviathan the coiling serpent;
he will slay the monster of the sea. [74]

Here we see the "serpent," or the volcano, and the "sword," the volcanic lightning that seems to destroy the volcano as it violently erupts.
Psalm 74:12-14,

But you, O God, are my king from of old;
you bring salvation upon the earth.
It was you who split open the sea by your power;
you broke the heads of the monster in the waters.
It was you who crushed the heads of Leviathan
and gave him as food to the creatures of the desert. [75]

Again we see God as the destroyer of the volcano that rose from the sea. Here are more references to volcanoes. [This is not an exhaustive list, but merely what I found on casual perusal; my comments and emphasis will be in brackets.] [76]:

- *Psalm 7:13*: He has prepared his deadly weapons; he makes ready his flaming arrows [lava bombs].
- *Psalm 11:5-6*: The LORD examines the righteous, but the wicked and those who love violence his soul hates. 6 On the wicked he will rain fiery coals [lava bombs] and burning sulfur [volcanic sulfur]; a scorching wind [volcanic outgassing] will be their lot.
- *Psalm 18:6-15*: I cried to my God for help. From his temple [volcano] he heard my voice; my cry came before him, into his ears. The earth trembled and quaked [volcanic earthquake], and the foundations of the mountains shook; they trembled because he was angry. Smoke rose from his nostrils [eruption]; consuming fire came from his mouth [magma flow], burning coals blazed out of it [lava bombs]. He parted the heavens and came down [fire from heavens seemed to come to

earth in the form of the volcano]; dark clouds [eruption ash] were under his feet. He mounted the cherubim [lava bombs] and flew; he soared on the wings of the wind. He made darkness his covering [volcanic ash cloud], his canopy around him — the dark rain clouds of the sky. Out of the brightness of his presence clouds advanced, with hailstones and bolts of lightning [volcanic lightning]. The LORD thundered from heaven; the voice of the Most High resounded [volcanic thunder]. He shot his arrows and scattered the enemies, great bolts of lightning, [volcanic lightning] and routed them. The valleys of the sea were exposed and the foundations of the earth laid bare at your rebuke, O LORD, at the blast of breath from your nostrils [sulfuric outgassing].

- *Psalm 18:46*: The LORD lives! Praise be to my Rock [volcano]!
- *Psalm 21:9*: At the time of your appearing you will make them like a fiery furnace [magma]. In his wrath the LORD will swallow them up [eruption], and his fire will consume them.
- *Psalm 29:7*: The voice of the LORD strikes with flashes of lightning [volcanic lightning].
- *Psalm 29:9-10:* And in his temple [volcano] all cry, "Glory!" [brilliance] The LORD sits enthroned over the flood [lava flow];
- *Psalm 30:*3 O LORD, you brought me up from the grave; you spared me from going down into the pit [caldera].
- *Psalm 30:9:* What gain is there in my destruction, in my going down into the pit [caldera].
- *Psalm 30:5*: For his anger [eruption] lasts only a moment, but his favor [fertile soil] lasts a lifetime;
- *Psalm 30:7:* O LORD, when you favored me, you made my mountain [volcano] stand firm...
- *Job 41:1-34:* [referring to the Leviatan] By his (sneezing) a light doth shine, and his eyes are like the eyelids of morning. Out of his mouth go burning lamps, and sparks of fire leap out. Out of his nostrils goeth smoke, as out of a seething pot or cauldron. His breath kindleth coals, and a flame goeth out of his mouth....His heart is as firm as a stone; yet, as hard as a piece of the nether millstone....He esteemeth iron as straw, and brass as rotten wood. The arrow cannot make him flee: slingstones are turned with him into stubble....He maketh the deep to boil like a pot....he is a king over all the children of pride.

The Tree of Life

The Cherubim were, according to legend, stationed near the Garden of Eden, to guard the Tree of Life. Magma rises from underground like a root, to branch forth as lava and from there to break down into rich soil and the inevitable plant and animal life. As I said, early humans observed this volcanic process and thought life came from the volcano, rather than from the seeds carried by birds. So a "tree of life" probably represents a volcano.

Here's *Genesis* 3:21-24 on the "tree of life" (not the "tree of knowledge" that was mentioned earlier in *Genesis*):

The LORD God made garments of skin for Adam and his wife and clothed them. And the LORD God said, 'The man has now become like one of us, knowing good and evil. He must not be allowed to reach out his hand and take also from the tree of life [volcano] and eat, and live forever.' So the LORD God banished him from the Garden of Eden to work the ground from which he had been taken. After he drove the man out, he placed on the east side (or placed in front) of the Garden of Eden cherubim [lava bombs] and a flaming sword flashing back and forth [volcanic lightning] to guard the way to the tree of life. [77]

Here we see God being concerned that man does not become immortal like the Gods (such as the Sun, Moon and the planets, that can regenerate by eating lava as they pass through the underworld when they dip "below" the horizon). The "flaming sword" is the volcanic lightning, which continues to flash as a volcano grows back little by little each year after being destroyed. This probably refers to Krakatau.

The snake symbolizes the magma-lava, as Osiris did in ancient Egypt. The tricky snake (lava snaking down the side of the volcano) did not want man and woman to achieve immortality. That was reserved for Osiris, feeding off the magma-lava, the food of the Gods.

So, the "tree of knowledge" represented a volcano that taught early humans about sulfur (which led to alchemy and then chemistry). Observations of the volcano led to the holistic and pervasive fire-earth-water-air model.

Jehovah

Jehovah is the God of the Old Testament and the Torah. The Hebrew God YHVH (also transliterated as YHWH, JHVH, JHWH, Yahwe, Yahveh, Yahve, Jahveh, Jahve, Jahweh, and Jahwe) was the unpronounceable sacred name of God or Jehovah. YHVH or later "Yaveh" or later "Jehovah," may be the same as the island, "Jawa" that later became "Java." "Java" or "Jawa" supposedly means "rice." However, on my trip to Indonesia in 1997, I found that Java could mean "fertility." This fertility probably refers to the rich volcanic soil.

YHWH (or "Yawa") originally may have been the sound that a volcano made as it outgassed carbon dioxide, water vapor and sulfurous gasses. Try pronouncing the letters YHWH. Do it slowly. The sound that you are making could easily be the sound of the gases that rise out of the volcanic area or the geological active area. What letters would you use to describe this sound? These letters fit quite well. ("Allah" may have a similar derivation.)

Jehovah seems to be referred to many times with volcanic-like characteristics. For example [my comments will be in brackets],

- *Exodus* 9:22-23: "and Jehovah gave thunder and hail [volcanic lightning and lava bombs], and the fire [lava] would run down to the earth, and Jehovah kept making it rain down hail [volcanic ash] upon the land of Egypt. Thus there came hail, and fire quivering in among the hail [small lava bombs]."
- *Exodus* 19:18: "And mount Si'nai smoked all over [eruptive ash], due to the fact that Jehovah came down upon it in fire [lava or lava bombs]; and its smoke kept ascending like the smoke of a kiln [volcanic ash cloud], and the whole mountain was trembling very much [volcanic tremors associated with rising magma]."
- *Deuteronomy* 4:33 we have: "Has any other people heard the voice of God speaking out [outgassing] of the middle of the fire the way you yourself have heard it and kept on living?"

This last statement, which sounds like the outgassing from a lava lake, such as near present day Ethiopia, where there has been a longstanding lava lake for 90 years.

My current research has revealed that there are no volcanoes along the Sinai Peninsula. However, perhaps the "voice of God" was the volcanic outgassing of carbon dioxide, water vapor and sulfurous gasses along the geological fault that runs through the island of Thera and then south along the length of the Sinai Peninsula. This fault may have been stirred by the famous eruption on Thera in 1628 BC.

Also, there may have been more travel than we are aware of in ancient times. The Bible talks of Solomon's fleet bringing gold from Ophir. Scholars are unsure of where this land lay. But in Sumatra I noticed there is an Ophir Mountain that still produces gold. This would fit with Bucky Fuller's (and other's) belief in ancient sea travel between the Orient and the Occident that he claims goes back at least 10,000 years.[78]

Many researchers now point to Thera as the primary cause of the many strange phenomena that occurred during the time of the exodus of the Jews from Egypt. In any case, *Jehovah was originally a volcano and keeps his volcanic characteristics throughout the Exodus of the Hebrews from Egypt.*

Sigmund Freud concurs.[79] As I stated earlier, in *Moses and Monotheism,* he writes, "Jahve was certainly a volcano-god."[80] He believed that the volcanic mountains on the western border of Arabia were the influential ones, and that Moses was the mediator between the volcano-god and the people.

The *Book of Genesis* says that God created man "in his own image." A scientifically minded person would not normally think of God as looking like *Homo sapiens*. So perhaps this puzzling phrase simply means that man (as well as all living things) was created from the lava-soil-dust of the Volcano God. Certainly upon viewing the "child of Krakatau" and seeing the ecosystem establishing itself there, one would begin to think that somehow living things were created out of the dust and soil of the volcano.

The Book of Geological Revelation

John's *Book of Revelation,* in the Christian New Testament manuscript, which describes a supposed worldwide cataclysm, is filled with volcanic imagery. However, to people of Europe (and eventually the United States), who have never seen a volcano explode, especially one explode like Krakatau, this book has been interpreted as a metaphorical description of the might of the Invisible God. Let me give some samples:

Revelation 8:8: "And something like a great mountain burning with fire was hurled onto the sea. And a third of the sea became blood."

Revelation 9:2: "And he opened the pit of the abyss, and smoke ascended out of the pit as the smoke of a great furnace, and the Sun was darkened, also by air, by the smoke of the pit."

John goes on (16:1) to talk of "seven angels" who pour their "seven bowls of anger of God" onto the earth. Then, among other things, (16:18) "lightnings and voices and thunders occurred and a great earthquake occurred such as had not occurred since men came to be on the earth, so extensive an earthquake, so great." In fact, he later says, (17:9) "Here is where wisdom comes in: *The seven heads mean seven mountains* ..." [my emphasis] We can see here what could easily be references to an ancient volcanic destruction. These seven mountains were perhaps seven large, active volcanoes of Java, Sumatra or the Virunga Range in Africa. They were probably linked to the seven sources of light in the ancient sky: Sun, Moon, Mercury, Venus, Mars, Jupiter, Saturn.

These were the only lights in the sky that didn't move with the rest of the stars or "firmament." (Although now we know that the Sun is a star and that the Moon shines only by its reflection.) Evidently, the ancient holistic (holy) theory attempted to unify the lights of the volcano (fire-mountain) to the lights of the heavens.

The ancient Maya calendar ends its cycle on 4 Ahau 3 Kankin (December 23, 2012). Many "prophets" of "doom and gloom" have sprung up in the United States, most recently in the Christian Apocalyptic movement. Likewise, Edgar Cayce predicted that around the year 2000 major cataclysms would occur in the western United States and Japan. Of course, they never occurred.

Predictions of catastrophe are echoes of more ancient ones. They are probably echoes of volcanic explosions or geologically induced tsunamis. Of course, early humans could not predict that far into the future. The point is that they were probably trying to predict when the next volcanic explosion would occur.

In fact, is it possible that the catastrophes these people and texts referred to had *already happened?* Could some of these predictions of destruction have referred to the next eruption-explosion of Krakatau? Alternatively, could they have referred to the next geologically induced tsunami?

If the ancient people did make these predictions from the observations of tens of thousands of years, and then passed them down orally or in writing, it was to protect us, the future generations. It is noteworthy that, *we still didn't get the message!* Thirty-six thousand people died in the Sunda strait in 1883 and over two hundred thousand in 2004! *This was despite the fundamentalist Christians, Moslems and Jews, etc., who insist on the sacred nature of their writings, who insist on the importance of their writings, and who are even willing in some cases to die for these writings.*

The point I am making is that fundamentalists are fiercely loyal to *mis*interpretations of their writings. The correct action would have been for them to be loyal to the correct meaning of the writings, which was: "The volcano is going to explode again! So beware and be ready to evacuate!" Alternatively: "There is going to be another big tsunami someday so be ready for it!"

When the magma chambers beneath Krakatau emptied, the caldera collapsed, and this collapse is what caused the huge explosion and the death of 36,000 in 1883. When the tectonic plates shifted near Sumatra in 2004 a massive tsunami was triggered which killed over 225,000.

Glory

"Glory" is a word that can mean light, halo or splendor. It is definitively associated with brightness, but also heaviness. To early humans it may have been the brightness (and heaviness) of the lava of the volcano. Exodus 24:17: "To the Israelites the glory of the LORD looked like a consuming fire on top of the mountain." In other words, God's glory may have originally been the volcano's light. (As we saw earlier, one of the few natural lights available to ancient minds.)

The Cross

As I said in an earlier chapter, the ankh was a symbol for regeneration and enduring life, which matches the constantly regenerating volcano. The ankh (formerly in use by Egyptians) is probably a representation of a volcano rising above the land or ocean. Although some think that the Christian cross derives from astrology, I think it more likely that it derives from the ankh of the Nile River Civilization. The cross symbol is used in several pagan religions. So the ancient symbol of the cross (currently in use by Christians) may be a representation of a volcano.

Caduceus drawing by author.

The caduceus is a stick that was carried by Mercury, the messenger of the Gods.

This symbol is similar to the cross and ankh, though which came first I am not sure. The two snakes around the center pole represent the magma flowing up from below, and the wings on the top represent the flying potential of the lava as lava bombs. As we said earlier, a messenger of the Gods was probably a lava bomb. (Also the caduceus is a symbol of the medical profession, so we see the beginnings of medical knowledge dating back to volcanoes.)

If you wanted to represent a volcano symbolically, how would you do it? An Ankh or cross would work well. (Also a triangle, as appears in Judaism, would most likely be a representation of a pyramid or volcano.)

It is known that the Romans did not crucify people on a cross, but on an upright stake or pole. A volcano represented resurrection, life, the creation of life, fire, knowledge, etc. By putting Jesus on a cross he was linked to this primitive and powerful symbol. (We see the same clever association when Buddha is pictured sitting on a volcanic island or serpents.) Thus the periodic and real resurrection of a volcano became the resurrection of man. Just as the Aztecs anthropomorphized (made-into-human) their volcano, so has Christianity. The volcanoes of the Old Testament have been replaced by a Man-God on a volcanic cross.

Many scholars question whether Jesus existed as a historical figure.[81] The term "Osiris-Dionysus" is a term used to refer to Mediterranean "life-death-rebirth" deities. The "historicity of Jesus" is a study beyond the scope of this book, however it would fit the themes of this book quite well if his character had been composed from earlier myths, which were composed from even earlier myths of ancient volcanic explosions and resurrections.

So when I see a "cross" now as I drive through the city or countryside, I see a symbol of a volcano (that which has given us life and that which has taken life), having been usurped by religion. I understand why this symbol has been used by religions, but I question the legitimacy of those who use it.

I also think of the 36,000 people who died at Krakatau in 1883, and the 225,000 who died in 2004. I think of all the people who may die in the many volcano eruptions that are still to come. I think of the huge volcanic eruption waiting to happen beneath Yellowstone Park.

The Judgment Day of the ancient text was not a nuclear war with a host of winged angels, led by Jesus in a chariot to raise the dead. Rather, it was the volcanic explosions and tsunamis that the early humans witnessed and tried to warn us about. Yes, a "host of angels" will come forth, *as lava bombs that pepper the countryside*, and yes, the dead may rise again, but not as individual personalities; rather they would rise as *billions of atoms* recycling into the atmosphere and soil, as the volcano spews forth all those animals long buried and decomposed in the ground. This is the accurate meaning of the "sacred" teachings.

All the crosses that surround us in predominately Christian countries, should be reminding us of the future volcanic threats.

4 ☼

The Volcano Gods

> *The Aztecs, Mayans and Quechuas offered human sacrifices to volcanoes, and until recently so did the peoples of many other volcanic areas.*
>
> Dorothy Vitaliano, Geologist

Ring of Fire

Southern California is part of the "Ring of Fire." The Ring of Fire is the outside edge of the huge Pacific plate (or upside down bowl), which is a slowly rotating plate of the Earth's crust under the Pacific Ocean. As a result of this rotation, in many millions of years Los Angeles will be next to San Francisco. The Ring creates the volcanoes and earthquakes of Central America South America and Chile, the earthquakes we have in Los Angeles, the volcanoes of the Pacific Northwest, including Mt. Saint Helena and Mt. Rainer, the volcanoes and earthquakes of Alaska, the volcanoes of the Kamchatka Peninsula, the volcanoes and earthquakes of Japan, the volcanoes of the Philippines and so on around the Ring.

I have experienced several earthquakes of more than seven on the Richter Scale. It is a terrifying experience to be in bed at night, on the third floor of an apartment building, and suddenly feel the floor and walls start to shake violently.

The Volcano Gods

You get dressed, you go outside, and you meet some of your neighbors. They also feel safer in the street.
You talk quietly,
"That was the strongest shake I've ever felt. Must've been an 8.0."
"I heard it was only 7.3."
"Well, it sure felt like an 8.0"
Someone has a radio and you listen to reports coming in from various parts of the city. Some damage here, no damage there. One man killed there. Several injured somewhere else. Eventually, you return to your bed. You wonder about the forces beneath your feet that could make the ground shake as if it were wet bread, and you don't sleep well that night. You feel there's a living monster beneath the Earth.
In the next few weeks, church attendance climbs in the city.

Volcanism was responsible for a large percentage of the land masses of the Earth. It was prevalent in ancient times. In Italy, human footprints were found in volcanic ash dated at 350,000 years ago.[82] In Africa, footprints have been found dated at 3.6 million years old.

Just since the last ice age (in the last 10,000 years) there have been "5,564 identifiable eruptions by the 1,343 known volcanoes."[83] Volcanoes are noticed especially on flights from the U.S. to Asia that pass over Alaska and Kamchatka. "More than 80 commercial aircraft have unexpectedly encountered volcanic ash in flight and at airports in the past 15 years. Seven of these encounters caused in-flight loss of jet engine power, which nearly resulted in the crash of the airplane."[84]

India

India is not far from Indonesia, whose extensive volcanic activity probably has influenced India. Also, there are several volcanic islands between Indonesia and India that were undoubtedly noticed by early seafarers, especially during a large eruption that produced a rising ash cloud seen for many miles. Additional island volcanoes are in the Indian Ocean near Madagascar.

When the ancient texts of Hinduism are read from a geological standpoint they make good sense. Most have been wrongly interpreted as modern-day rockets or flying machines. Make an Internet search on "Vimānas" and you will be amazed at how these geological descriptions have been misinterpreted as spaceships, etc. For example, here's a description of Arjuna's chariot:

58

The Volcano Gods

The chariot had all necessary equipment. It could not be conquered by gods or demons, and it radiated light and reverberated with a deep rumbling sound. Its beauty captivated the minds of all who beheld it. Visvakarma, the lord of design and creation had created it by the power of his austerities, and its form, like that of the sun, could not be precisely discerned.[85]

The light, the sound and the vague form all point to a lava bomb not a spaceship.

The Ramayana tells the story of how Rama, Lakshman and the monkey army built a bridge from the tip of India to Sri Lanka and then crossed over to Lanka.[86] This is a way of remembering that Sri Lanka at one time was connected to India, before the ocean level rose at the end of the last ice age. It's worth detailing some things about the battle between Rama (the volcanic lightning) and ten-headed Ravana (the erupting volcano) as they so closely parallel our chapter on Ancient Egypt and Mott Green's analysis of Greece. [My comments will be in brackets.]

The Battle Between Rama and Ravana[87]

Ravana was also ready in his huge chariot ... Conches and trumpets were blown [volcanic rumblings], and the sound generated terror in the hearts of the opponents ... Ravana had ten heads [volcanic vents] which he had obtained as boon for his special worship of God [fire-magma] ... It was also suggestive of long life [volcanic life], every head was compatible with life. Rama and Ravana hurled missiles [lightning from Rama but lava bombs from Ravana] at each other. Both were able to counter opponent's attacks. When one head of Ravana rolled down, it was replaced by a new one! [volcanic regeneration]. If one arm of Ravana was cut, it was replaced by another! [volcanic regeneration]. It was impossible to kill this powerful Rakshasa (demon).

Then Rama destroyed Ravana's chariot. But, instead of falling on the ground Ravana flew high in the sky and started attacking Rama and his men with arrows and maces [lava bombs], and dropped magical fire [ash falls or pyroclastic flows] and stones [lava bombs]. Moreover, he took multiple forms [multiple vents] to terrorize Rama's army. Some forms were having only head, while others were composed of trunks only! [flank eruptions of parasitic vents]. This "Mayawi Yuddha" — Illusory War—posed additional pressure on Rama to select the original Ravana [central vent] and hit him. The energy was drained out from the tiring army men. Arrows and missiles [lightning bolts] made no impact on Ravana in the least. Many of the monkeys and bears from Rama's army were disheartened. They were tired and many tried to escape the rain of arrows and fire [lava bombs] being poured [outflowed] by Ravana. Rama protected all his men by counter attacks [volcanic lightning] and by providing special cover against Ravana's attacks.

The Volcano Gods

Laxmana, Hanuman, Angad, Sugreeva and Jambuwanta all tried their own missiles on mighty Ravana but in vain. When the arrow of Rama [volcanic lightning] failed how could any other succeed!

The day turned into night [the eruption cloud covered the Sun], and both the armies retreated to their respective camps [a lull in the eruption]. The injured were treated with potions and ointments. Rama and Laxmana with their associates discussed the way and means to put an end to Ravana. But no definite answer could be had as Ravana was adept in this kind of war games. Moreover, he had the capacity to regenerate any lost part of the body [volcanic resurrection]. Death of Ravana was difficult to imagine!

However, Vibhishana remembered something about his brother, Ravana, that had a great bearing on the outcome of war. He recalled how he once had faintly overheard the weakness in the body of Ravana — and that weak spot was his umbilicus (middle abdominal region) [central vent], not head, nor heart, nor neck! If Rama could hit the arrowhead [volcanic lightning] in that localized spot, the life-sustaining nectar [magma or soma] would spill and Ravana was sure to die.

Thus, armed with the special knowledge, next day, Rama put an end to Ravana's life with the arrow in his naval [volcanic lightning at the climactic explosion]. The mightiest king on the earth [the volcano] fell [volcanic collapse and caldera creation]. This brought to an end clanging of weapons [volcanic noise] and associated bitterness and ill feelings. The injured Ravana was counting his last breaths [sulfuric outgassing]. Mandodari came rushing to her injured husband with eyes full of tears and heart filled with unexplainable pathos. Rama went to her and consoled the lady with soft words of sympathy [gentle breeze]. He also gave her advice about the impermanence of life and reality of death as the only truth after birth. He proclaimed to her and all the people around that Ravana will be remembered for eternity for his good [fertile volcanic soil] as well as bad deeds [lava flows, lava bombs, pyroclastic flows].

Then turning to Laxmana Rama said, "O dear brother, look the mighty Ravana is lying on his death bed. His knowledge of Vedas and Scripture is beyond doubt [being the nexus of the underworld and the atmosphere, early humans assumed that the volcano God had an understanding of nature]. But equally true is the fact that you will not find more knowledgeable authority on politics, statesmanship, and sociology on the earth today. Please go and get the knowledge from him. [Early humans using nature as a guide as to how humans should act.]

Thus Laxmana, sitting at the feet of Ravana, learnt many useful things on diplomacy, politics, tax structure, social reforms, war preparedness and many more from him. When Ravana breathed his last [final outgassing], Rama himself conducted the last rites befitting the grandeur of Brahmin Rakshasa King.

In this story, we see not only the volcanic lightning, which destroys the volcano (as in the case of Hesiod's Mediterranean volcanoes and also the Egyptian descriptions), but also the fact of early humans learning from volcanoes. As I said earlier, the magicians (alchemists) learned from studying the sulfur compounds, which are the prime components of fire-powder and an important element in chemistry.

The book *Mythology*,[88] edited by Cavendish contains some pertinent information about Hinduism, which I will use in this next section, as I develop my theory regarding Soma and volcanic correspondences. [I put the volcanic correspondences in brackets]:

Hindu texts mention the "navel of the earth" [as blood flows to the new born baby through the umbilical cord so does lava flow to the earth through the volcano]. The "golden seed" of the god Prajapati developed into a "golden egg" which split in two [underwater lava appears to split open like an egg].

Prajapati was not completely immortal. Half (the hair, skin, flesh, bone and marrow) was mortal, and the other half (mind, voice, breath, eye, and ear) was immortal. [This is partially correct in that it is an attempt to show that the body, which seemed to disappear into the air upon cremation, is about 65% oxygen. This will be more fully discussed later.]

Vritra is a great serpent [magma] that lies coiled about the world-mountain [a volcano, possibly Krakatau] at the navel [place where lava sustenance is provided] of the earth, holding back the waters [liquid lava or tidal wave]. The sun was held fast in the underworld night [volcanic ash blocks out the Sun].

Indra, the king of the Gods, [corresponding to Seth, Zeus, Rama and volcanic lightning] pierces Vritra, a serpent or dragon, and lets loose the cows (symbols of wealth and fertility) and releases the sun. Indra is also said to have cut off the wings of the mountain, which were flying about and causing great destruction [lava bombs].

Tvashtar is often said to be Indra's father. Indra kills Tvashta, as he had been hiding the Soma, the elixir of immortality.

The Gods are said to have obtained immortality by drinking Soma. *I believe that Soma was originally not some plant or mushroom as is generally believed, but originally was magma and lava.* In Hymn XCI we read: "These herbs, these milch-kine (milk cows), and these running waters, all these, O Soma, thou hast generated. The spacious firmament hast thou expanded, and with the light thou hast dispelled the darkness."

This is quite similar to the Horus-kills-Osiris myth and may have the same origin. *The lava seems to give immortality by forever rejuvenating or resurrecting the volcano.* After drinking Soma [magma] the Gods could live their full life span of a thousand years [the time until another violent eruption]. "Soma" is related to the word "to press out." The Indo-European root word is related to "swelling" and "swollen." The swelling volcano seemed to press out the liquid food of the Gods.

Soma is frequently compared to a cow. Indra milked this cow. The volcano was like a cow's teat.

The heavens of Indra are thought to need the sacred food from the cow's teat or volcano: "Who milketh out this mighty Pair, the Earth and Heaven, like mother kine [cow] All-bounteous art thou in carouse [to drink fully]. Who in a moment mightily floweth around these two world-halves: All-bounteous art thou in carouse."[89] Later, "Hath he [Indra] not, purified, impregned the kine [volcano] who long to meet their Lord, The kine who yield the shining milk [magma]?"[90] In other words, imagine Indra, in the sky, sucking nourishment from the volcano, or cow's teat.

A sieve is frequently mentioned. A sieve separates larger particles from smaller ones. This is perhaps commenting on the fact that the large lava boulders eventually break down into smaller and smaller ones and eventually pebbles and soil.

"The meath [sweet liquor] is offspring of thy sap: All-bounteous art thou in carouse."[91] This refers to the fact that all sweet things eventually grow out of the soil that the Soma has broken down into.

The early humans were looking at the worlds of Heaven and Earth and trying to describe it as best they could. If you read the *Rig Veda* from a geological viewpoint, it makes good sense. However, as I said, first you must try to see the world as they saw it.

Tibet

Mandala: The mandala is "a schematized representation of the cosmos, chiefly characterized by a concentric configuration of geometric shapes, each of which contain an image of a deity or an attribute of a deity."[92] It is prevalent in Tibet, and probably originally represented a volcano. As Bucky Fuller describes in *Tetrascroll* and *Critical Path,* all the great rivers of Asia lead up into Tibet. Tibet is the Source. Early humans, most likely evolving/ differentiating near the ocean, followed these fresh water rivers up to their source. Fresh water was vital to them. They brought with them the knowledge they had learned of seamounts that emerged from the ocean to become volcanoes.

The Mandala was the unfolding of the cosmic order; in other words, lava making land and life. Mandala was not a psychological construct until Jung tried to make it one. Originally, "Before the meditating person arrives at the gates, she must, however, pass the four outer circles: the purifying fire of wisdom, the vajra [thunderbolt of one of the Gods] circle, the circle with the eight tombs and the lotus circle."[93]

In Tibetan art one can see many serpents beneath the ground. One can see many fiery devils, which, over time, are merged with more dignified Buddha images. Somewhat like in Christianity, Buddha was absorbed within the ancient volcano worship.

Shambhala: This is a concept in Tibetan religion. "For thousands of years rumors and reports have circulated that somewhere beyond Tibet, among the icy peaks and secluded valleys of Eurasia, there lies an inaccessible paradise, a place of universal wisdom and ineffable peace called Shambhala – although it is also known by other names."[94]

"In the mythology of Pon, the native religion of Tibet, Shambhala was a Central Asian kingdom, the origin and center of the world whence issued all spiritual energies."[95] Here is the yogi El Morya (died in late 1800s) on Shambhala. Note the volcanic themes:

The Ruler of Shambhala is the fiery Impeller of Life and of the Fire of the Mother of the World. His Breath is ablaze with flame and His Heart is aglow with the fire of the Silvery Lotus. The Ruler of Shambhala lives and breathes in the Heart of the Sun. The Ruler of Shambhala is the Invoker and the Invoked. The Ruler of Shambhala is the Sender of the Arrow and the Receiver of all arrows. The Ruler of Shambhala breathes the Truth and affirms the Truth. The Ruler of Shambhala is invincible, turning destruction into construction.[96]

Middle and South America

There are numerous references to volcanoes throughout the literature of the Aztecs and the Mayans. These writings now can be examined and clearly understood by using the volcanic/geologic paradigm.

The pyramid at Chichen Itza in the Yucatan is oriented so that at the equinoxes, in the spring and fall, the sunlight and shadows create the "image of a serpent slithering down the northern staircase of the pyramid."[97] The pyramids of Middle America, like those of the Nile River, were representation of these volcanoes. The many references to serpents (or snakes), as with the Nile River civilization, were again references to the lava.

The Aztecs used to sacrifice their human victims on the top of pyramids.[98] They were attempting to mimic, with blood, the red lava flowing of the volcano. (Some volcanoes are "pulsating volcanoes" in that they will outflow lava on a regular schedule, such as every 20 minutes.) The Aztecs may have thought that the volcano was like a human heart.

The architecture and art of the area also reflects the volcanic nature of the region. Go into any museum with artifacts from this region of the world and you will see many bizarre looking creatures that are representations of the twisted and hardened lava, and also many artifacts concerned with incense burning that reflect the smoking volcanoes. I have seen this in the Natural History museum in Los Angeles and in the Southwestern Museum.

Two main gods were Quetzalcoatl and Tezcatlipoca:

Quetzalcoatl, the plumed (feathered) serpent, probably represents the magma of the volcano, like Osiris in Egypt. These plumes or feathers are representative of the flickering flames of fire. Quetzalcoatl was known to have created fire for humanity. In one story, "To atone for great sins, Quetzalcoatl threw himself onto a funeral pyre, where his ashes rose to the heavens as a flock of birds carrying his heart to the star Venus."[99] This is quite similar to the destruction of a volcano.

Tezcatlipoca probably represented volcanic lightning, like Seth in Egypt or Zeus in Greece. His name comes from "shining smoke,"[100] which probably refers to the shining smoke of the volcano as the lightning flashes. One aspect of Tezcatlipoca ruled over darkness, terrible cold, volcanic eruptions and disaster.[101]

Tezcatlipoca was "associated with the forces of evil and destruction. Tezcatlipoca shared dominion over humanity with Quetzalcoatl, the god of light and good. Of the various legends surrounding their continual feud, one of the most important tells of Quetzalcoatl's expulsion from Tula, the Toltec capital."[102] Note the parallels with the Egyptian story: the continual feud, the expulsion of one god (or explosion in the case of Osiris), and the destructive elements for both Seth and Tezcatlipoca.

Here is a story about Tezcatlipoca from South America, from the Nahuas. [my comments will be in brackets]

Tezcatlipoca, god of the four quarters, was enraged! From the farrest corners and the deepest depths he launched forth swarms of blackened clouds [eruption cloud of volcanic ash] spun 'round and ripped through with his lightning lash [volcanic lightning]. Flashing and rumbling [volcanic lightning and thunder] they besieged the Mansion of the Sun [volcano and magma]. From the endless deeps of his throat [the crater] roared black thunder [ash and volcanic rumbling], and everything round about crumbled [central cone collapse]. The Sun was caught up in the seething blackness [ash] in the sky, a bleary redness in the dark.[103]

Here is another pertinent story [my comments]:

Tlaltecuhtli (Earth Lord) was a large earth monster [volcano] in Aztec mythology described as female, who desires flesh and has mouths [parasitic vents] at her elbows, knees, and other joints.

According to the Histoyre du Mechique, Tezcatlipoca and Quetzalcoatl agree that they can't continue with their re-creation of the world with her around, so they decide to destroy her. Transforming into two great serpents, one snake seizes her left hand and right foot while the other seizes her right hand and left foot. They then rip the monster apart - her upper body becoming the earth and her lower half is thrown into the sky to create the heavens [volcanic explosion].

This act of violence angers the other gods, and in order to console the earth, it is decided that all plants needed for human life will be created out of her body [lava breakdown into fertile soil]. The trees, flowers, & herbs come from her hair [rope lava]. The grasses and smaller flowers come form her skin. The mountain ridges and valleys are made from her nose [lava weathering]. Her eyes become the source of wells, springs and small caves, while her mouth becomes the source for great rivers and caverns [lava weathering]. It is said she still screams for blood [magma] during the night & can only be soothed with sacrificial flesh and blood.[104]

From another source on the two gods: "On the one hand, they work together in creating the Earth and the Heavens; while on the other hand, they are constantly hostile to each other. They seem to be forever trying to destroy one another and they usually succeed, though Tezcatlipoca is usually more victorious."[105] Note how the feuding creates the Earth, which matches the volcanic creation stories of Egypt. Also, note how the new volcanic land or island becomes populated with trees, plants, etc.

Quetzalcoatl is associated with the underworld, as was Osiris. "After the destruction of the Fourth Sun, Quetzalcoatl descends into the underworld ... After enduring certain trials inflicted on him by the god of death, he retrieves the bones and ashes of the previous humanity that are needed to make the new one."[106] We see here the chemical decomposition of the body and "creation of humanity," or "reincarnation," as it was assumed that the humans appeared on the volcanic land due to creation.

Here is an interesting quote about Quetzalcoatl: "He was

never dressed but in a robe of white cotton, well girded to the body and so large that it covered the feet, for greater modesty."[107] This "robe of white" reminds me of the "white crown" of Osiris. Remember the white sulfur deposits of Krakatau? Mexico's most famous volcano is Popocatepetl (smoking mountain). At the top are white sulfur deposits! According to the now dead volcanologists[108] Katia and Maurice Krafft: "When the Spaniards conquered Mexico, Cortez dispatched an expedition to bring back sulfur with which to make gunpowder for his siege of Tenochtitlan. Aztec Indians were lowered into the crater in search of the sulfur deposits."[109]

Furthermore, there is a story that Quetzalcoatl was a "white man" who would return someday. When Cortez came ashore he was thought to be the returned god by the Aztecs. If we simply change this "white man" to "white skin," and we remember that volcanoes have a tendency to return, or become active again, or be replaced by another volcano (the son), then we can understand the origins of this myth. White skin translates to sulfur deposits, and the "return" is the regeneration of the volcano from the magma chambers below.

Unfortunately for the Aztecs, they anthropomorphized (made-into-a-person) their volcano. They had lost touch with the true origins of their myths: nature. Most cultures today also have lost touch.

In this story of Cortez and his conquest of he Aztecs, we see a reoccurring theme: early humans develop their science and then pass it along orally (or later by writing) and declare it to be very important (sacred). The culture then passes it along in an abstract and robotic fashion, making school children memorize it for their daily lessons. The culture has, in essence, lost the meaning of their knowledge.

This corruption of knowledge probably has resulted in the loss of many thousands of lives from volcanic explosions or the resulting tidal waves (floods). Meanwhile, religious fundamentalists loudly proclaim the importance of their "sacred texts," which they do not even dimly grasp.

Who is to blame for this? Is it just ignorance? Is it greed and maliciousness? Is it some combination of these two?

China

As early as 300 BC there are references to what are called "dragon bones," (which were of course dinosaur bones). The geologically active Ring of Fire surrounds China's eastern coast. Prehistoric seafarers may have brought stories of these volcanoes to mainland China and the story of the fire-breathing dragon was born.

The Volcano Gods

A Chinese legend concerns creation: P'an-ku forming from a cosmic egg. (Another reference to the hatching egg shape that forms when lava meets water.) P'an-ku grew for 18,000 years at the rate of about 10 feet per day. (The same order of magnitude as the growth of a volcano.) From this the earth was made as well as the sky. (This is somewhat correct as most of the continents formed from lava, and the outgassing of steam and gas create the atmosphere.) The five great mountains come from his body, the rivers and seas from his blood and fluids, and the soil from his flesh.[110]

Another legend from China is told by Chuang-tzu, in the Third Century: Shu, the Emperor of the Northern Sea and Hu, the Emperor of the Southern Sea create the known world from Chaos. Their names together, shu-hu, mean lightning.

Chuang-tzu used these two words purposefully, it is believed, to "denote the truth that when the illumination from light strikes chaos, it leads to the creation of life and the restoration of order."[111] Here, again, we see an ancient awareness of volcanic lightning and the phreatomagmatic explosion, which leads to the collapse of the volcano and the resulting geologic stability.

Here's an illustrative telling of this creation story. Note the pouring out of lava and light. [my comments will be in brackets]:

> In the beginning, according to Chinese mythology, there was only a cosmic egg. Within it, amongst the swirling darkness of chaos, slept a giant called P'an Ku [magma], who had been developing for eighteen thousand years [growth of magma reservoir]. Upon awakening he smashed the egg [magma meeting sea water] and allowed the darkness to pour out, as well as light [magma-lava] that had been trapped within the chaos.
> The darkness fell and created earth, while fragments of light rose up [red hot ashes] and created heaven [volcanic outgassing]. Disturbed by the idea that chaos could return if the light and dark were to mix, P'an Ku set himself the task of keeping the earth and sky apart [as a volcano] until he could be sure all was safe.
> After tens of millennia P'an Ku decided that everything was okay - so he sank into the earth [volcanic collapse and caldera formation] and died. His final breath [outgassing] became the wind and clouds. His body and limbs formed the mountains and hills [lava weathered into soil], and his blood flowed as streams and rivers. Vegetation grew from his hair [rope lava], and his teeth gave us precious jewels [diamonds are frequently found near volcanoes]. P'an Ku created order out of chaos.[112] [Liquid lava into rigid earth.]

When I traveled through South East Asia I frequently saw statues of the Buddha meditating while seated on a large coil snake. I

The Volcano Gods

interpret this serpent as the magma/lava stream.

Northern Europe

In Norse, Thor was the same as Seth, Zeus and Tezcatlipoca.
Thor was the volcanic lightning that the Vikings saw when they traveled to Iceland. The seafaring Vikings witnessed the extensive and continuous volcanic activity along this mid-Atlantic ridge, which is a spreading ridge.

The myth of Raganarök is well known: Here are some excerpts [my comments will be in brackets]:

... the wolf will swallow the sun [black volcanic ash will block the Sun] ...The Stars will disappear from the heaven ... the whole surface of the earth and mountains will tremble [volcanic earthquakes] ...The sea will lash against the land because the Midgard Serpent [magma chamber] is writhing in giant fury [volcanic earthquakes] trying to come ashore. The wolf Fenrir ... his eyes and ears will blaze with fire [vents outflowing lava]. The Midgard Serpent will blow so much poison [hot ash and sulfuric outgassing] that the whole sky and sea will be splattered with it. [113]

After this: "the earth rises up from the sea again, and is green and beautiful and things grow without sowing."[114] Of course this is the lava breaking down into fertile soil.

Greece and Rome

As I mentioned in an earlier chapter, the Greeks had Zeus as their volcanic lightning and the Titans as volcanoes. We met Mott Greene earlier, in the chapter on Egypt, and presented his theory that the mega-eruption of Thera in 1628 BC is detailed in Hesiod's *Theogony*. In his book, *Natural Knowledge in Preclassical Antiquity*, Greene also goes into considerable detail concerning a second eruption immediately after Thera.

He notes that if myth is but literature, as many commentators have suggested, then this second eruption does not fit. "A drama may have but one climax ...There is something Sisyphean and un-lord-of-the-universe in Zeus having to unpack the thunderbolts twice in succession to vanquish the same sort of adversary."[115] Of course, if the myth represents the actual sequence of events in the natural world, then we cannot quibble with the ending. Greene goes on to provide evidence that this second event probably was an eruption of Mt. Etna in Sicily. For example, Etna has many parasitic cones (secondary or side vents). In Book 12 of the *Theogony,* Hesiod says, "A hundred snake heads grew from the shoulders of the terrible dragon, with black tongues flickering and fire flashing from the eyes."[116]

So again a battle wages:

[Zeus] thundered hard and strong, so that the earth and broad sky above, Sea and Ocean Streams, and the Tartarus region below the earth, all rumbled with the awful sound. Great Olympus quaked under the divine feet of its royal master as he rose up, and the earth groaned also ...

The heat from both sides, from the thunder and lightning of Zeus and from the fiery monster [lava jets] penetrated the violet deep and made the whole earth and sky and sea boil. The clash of those immortal beings made the long waves rage around the shores, round and about, starting a convulsion that would not stop.[117]

Green notes that shallow-focus earthquakes occur when the magma begins to rise up through the central vent from the reservoir miles below. Around Mt. Etna "jets of lava as high as 200 meters have been observed." Enormous amounts of gas are released leading to volcanic lightning.

When Zeus had risen to the peak he took his weapons, thunder and lightning and the smoking thunderbolt, and jumped on his antagonist from Olympus and struck. He blasted all those prodigious heads of the monsters and dealt him a flogging until he was tamed. Typhoeus fell down crippled, and the monstrous earth groaned underneath. Flame streamed from the once powerful potentate, now struck by lightning in the dim clefts of the rocky mountain where he fell. Large tracts of the monstrous earth were set on fire by the prodigious heat and melted like tin heated in moulded crucibles by skilled workmen, or like iron, the strongest metal softened by the heat of the fire in some mountain cleft, even so did the earth melt in the flame of the fire thus kindled.[118]

Greene says that while "literary" and other interpretations regard this as an imitation of the battle with the Titans, "... the text provides a one-for-one correspondence between the battle events and the eruptive signature of a known volcano, entirely distinct from any other in the Mediterranean world."[119] In other words, according to Greene, this passage confirms that the volcano is Etna.

We will now leave Mott Greene's analysis, and discuss a different Greek god, Prometheus. Here is a relevant passage:

Prometheus took some of this earth, and kneading it up with water, made man in the image of the gods ... Prometheus was one of the Titans [volcanoes], a gigantic race, who inhabited the earth before the creation of man ... Prometheus ... with the aid of Minerva, went up to heaven, and lighted his torch at the chariot of the sun and brought down fire to man.[120]

Here we see the volcano Prometheus creating man, much as the Divine Potter of ancient Egypt did. Also we see the Grand Unification Theory of the ancients: The fire of the volcano is explained as being similar in nature to the Sun by the fact of the volcano having taken it from the Sun.

As the myth goes, Zeus punished Prometheus for giving fire to man, was bound, and his liver was pecked out each day by an eagle, but then regenerated at night. If you have seen a volcano, you know that the dried lava looks somewhat like liver. The "eagle" may represent air erosion on the side of the volcano, while the "regeneration" refers to continuous lava flow, like the volcano Kilauea that I saw in Hawaii or the volcano Merapi that I saw on Java (which pumps out or pulsates lava regularly every 20 minutes). Zeus binds Prometheus because the erupting volcano that ceases to erupt would seem to be somehow "bound."

In another legend, Prometheus saves the human race from extinction by warning his son, Deucalion, of a great flood. Deucalion survives by taking refuge with his wife in a chest. (This of course is echoed in Christian writings of Noah.) I suggested in an earlier chapter that the "warning" is probably the rumbling that volcanoes make for several months before they violently erupt. The flood is the tidal wave caused by the exploding volcano. Here is an excerpt from the flood legend:

The mountains which the Greeks named Kaukosos, which is more than thirty thousand stadia distant from India; and here it was that they laid the scene of the story of Prometheus and of his being put in bonds; for these were the farthermost mountains towards the east that were known to writers of that time. And the expedition of Dionysos and Herakles to the country of the Indians looks like a mythical story of later date, because Herakles is said to have released Prometheus one thousand years later ... Prometheus was bound at the ends of the earth on the Kaukasos.[121]

This excerpt is interesting because it reminds me of Krakatau, which is at the "ends of the earth" to Mediterranean writers.

Next, let's examine the myth of Phaethon (the word is derived from "to shine") as told by Ovid in *Metamorphoses* in 7-8 AD.[122] [my comments will be in brackets]:

Phaethon [the magma-lava light] boasted that the Sun, Helios, was

70

The Volcano Gods

his father. When challenged about this he goes to the Palace of the Sun to ask the "universal light of the great world." There the Sun reassures him that he is indeed his son and to prove it will grant any favor to Phaethon. Phaethon wants to take his father's chariot, which, of course, moves the sun across the sky.

The Sun is displeased and says "no one but myself has the power to occupy the chariot of fire." He severely warns Phaethon even further but Phaethon persists until the Sun gives in. The horses of the chariot run wild until the dazed Phaethon lets go of the reins! [the violent eruption] The horses run amok and the "earth bursts into flame ... The meadows turn white, the trees are consumed with all their leaves, and the scorched corn makes its own destruction ... Great cities are destroyed with all their walls, and the flames reduce whole nations with all their peoples to ashes. The woodlands burn, with the hills."

Phaethon does not know where he is, or where he is going. Kindly Earth asks for help from Jupiter, the father of the gods: "the all-powerful father of the gods climbs to the highest summit of heaven, from where he spreads his clouds over the wide earth, from where he moves the thunder and hurls his quivering lightning bolts [volcanic lightning], calling on the gods, especially on him who had handed over the sun chariot, to witness that, unless he himself helps, the whole world will be overtaken by a ruinous fate ... He thundered, and balancing a lightning bolt in his right hand threw it from eye-level at the charioteer [more volcanic lightning], removing him, at the same moment, from the chariot and from life, extinguishing fire [magma] with fierce fire ... Phaethon, flames ravaging his glowing hair [tracers of lava bombs], is hurled headlong, leaving a long trail in the air, as sometimes a star does in the clear sky, appearing to fall although it does not fall." Phaethon dies.

This myth is frequently misinterpreted as advice to a father about giving in to the son's wishes. If you have been reading closely you see the similarities to the Greek myth mentioned in the chapter on Egypt. Phaethon here would be the magma-lava, or like Osiris, God of the underworld.

The search for a Unified Theory would make the ancients wonder about the connection between the Sun and lava. They intuitively felt they must be connected and so developed a cognitive map of what happens during a volcanic eruption (the wild chariot ride) when lava bombs are flying every which way. Seth is replaced by Jupiter and, just like in ancient Egypt, he saves the day by hurling lightning. The phenomenon of volcanic lightning (as elaborated in a chapter on Egypt) explains things quite well.

Some writers interpret this as a comet description, but this is not the best interpretation. The glowing hair is not a comet's tail, but hot ashes that trail behind the lava bombs as they streak through the air.

Comets crashing into the Earth are extremely rare and so catastrophic that people usually wouldn't know what hit them. Early

71

humans would not be able to examine comet impacts repeatedly and closely as they would with a volcano. In science, the simplest theory that explains the results is the best. A volcanic theory is much simpler than the comet impact explanation of myths. Also the extremely close correspondence with the Egyptian story and other stories, makes it most likely that Phaethon was not a comet, but a volcano.

Ovid (43 BC-17 AD) tells the story of a great flood that Jupiter sent to destroy mankind. Only Deucalion and his wife Pyrrha are saved. His description sounds like a volcanic explosion followed by a tidal wave. The volcanic tidal wave is made to seem like rain at times, but at other times it appears to be clearly a great wave.

Before we leave the Greeks and Romans, here are some comments on Ambrosia and the Chimera:

Ambrosia: the food of the gods. The word ambrosia literally means "immortality." What the early humans saw as immortal were the regenerating volcanoes. Ambrosia was probably magma. This was what "regenerated" the volcano and thus what made the Gods seem immortal. Ambrosia was the ancient Greek equivalent of Soma.

Chimera: A monster with the head of a lion, body of a goat and the tail of a dragon (or sometimes said to be a serpent). It breathed fire and devastated the land of Lycia (in the southwest corner of Asia Minor) until Bellerophon killed it.[123] He "was able to capture and tame the winged horse Pegasus, with whose help he was able to slay the Chimera, by riding on its back across the sky and beheading the creature."[124]

Here we see Bellerophon taking the place of Zeus or Seth. "Riding the back" of the volcano, and "beheading it." After it explodes, a volcano appears beheaded. (This was like when Mt. Saint Helena exploded in Oregon in 1980.) The volcanic lightning of Zeus or Seth, which bolts down into the throat of the volcano, even while clear skies surround it for miles, would make it seem like the God was "riding" the volcano.

Arabia

Ka'ba: "The wall of the Ka'ba, the holiest shrine of Islam at Mecca contains a black stone that has been reported to be of meteoritic origin. A silver band holds the stone, which measures 16 by 20 cm. together. Legend has it that the angel Gabriel gave the stone to the patriarch Abraham who built it into his house. The stone passed to the prophet Mohammed who built it into the wall of the Ka'ba."[125] Of course if an "angel" gave it to him, then it may be a lava bomb, not a meteor fragment.

The Volcano God Theory

In this chapter, I gave additional supporting evidence for my proposal that volcanism and geological phenomena were one of the two most important considerations in the establishment of ancient science-religion. A much more detailed analysis and reconstruction could be done, but as I said earlier, my aim is to provide an overarching theory. I am quite confident that this theory is correct.

This geological interpretation can be applied to the "mythologies" of the ancient Mayans and Aztecs, the Chinese, the Indians, the Norse, the Greeks, Babylonians, the Jews and Christians, the alchemists and others. My research suggests that ancient people all over the world observed geological phenomena such as volcanoes and formalized this knowledge in their "myths," which were really a proto-science.

The legend of the "Flood," contained in many ancient traditions, probably derived from something like the tsunami that killed 36,000 people in 1883 at Krakatau, or 225,000 people in 2004, also from a geological event in Indonesia. In a more ancient volcanic explosion, a person (perhaps named Noah) may have correctly interpreted the pre-explosive rumblings of the volcano as meaning that it was about to explode and so he built a ship.

By this point in my research, I had realized an important fact: geology can be a unifying principle in mythology, just as evolution is a unifying principle in biology.

5 ☼

Geological Creation and Destruction

> *While we debate the nature of myth we must remain forthrightly attuned to the real existence of myths of nature.*
>
> Professor Mott T. Greene

Mythological Surveys

In his book, *Eden in the East,* Steven Oppenheimer reviews the myths of the world: "After the watery chaos, separation—usually of the Sky from the Earth—is the next most commonest theme in cosmogonic [world origin] myths."[126] He calls this the "Creation Story of Separation" and documents its use in the Americas, Africa, Europe, Jew/Arab/Phoenicia, Mesopotamia, Central Asia-Siberia, Indo-Iran, Japan, China-Tibet, Southeast Asia, Indonesia, Melanesia, Micronesia, Polynesia, and Aboriginal Australia.

He says there are 10 recurring motifs in these stories (some occurring more frequently in certain areas than others): water-dragon, light, creative word, separation of heaven and earth, parricide, use of body (to build the earth, etc.), creative wind, sevens, creator incest, and cosmic egg.[127] Oppenheimer does not realize it, but most of these fit nicely within a volcanic paradigm.

75

The "water-dragon" would be the rising volcano such as Thera or Krakatau. The "light" is the light that appears from the volcano and is the unified light of the universe. The "separation of heaven and earth" is the volcano creating the land and the atmosphere (outgassing) and appearing to create the lights in the sky. "Parricide" we have seen in the Osiris-Horus myth, in which the newer, younger volcano appears to have "killed" the older one. The "use of the body" to build earth is obvious in several of the myths I have presented. The "Tree of Life" we mentioned in another chapter as representing a volcano. The "Waters of Life" would be the magma and lava, not water. (The "creative wind" will be discussed extensively later.) The "cosmic egg" we have discussed as the shape created by underwater lava flows.

In the book *When They Severed Earth from Sky: How the Human Mind Shapes Myth* the authors also present evidence that mythology has a foundation in the natural world. They show that a certain Native American myth was caused by a Crater Lake (Oregon) volcanic eruption 7,675 years ago. [128]

Here's a creation story from the ancient Finish *Kalevala*, which uses the cosmic egg motif:

> From the cracked egg's lower fragment,
> Now the solid earth was fashioned,
> From the cracked egg's upper fragment,
> Rose the lofty arch of heaven,
> From the Yolk, the upper portion,
> Now became the sun's bright luster;
> From the white, the upper portion,
> Rose the moon that shines so brightly. [129]

In *Hamlet's Mill*, another fairly comprehensive survey of the world's myths, we find the authors linking a whirlpool with the Tree of Life. "The basic scheme works in many parts of the world...it is as if the particular waters hidden below tree, pillar, or mill's axle waited only for the moment when someone should *removed that plug*." (My emphasis.) The authors give many examples: Rama is going to shoot his magical arrow into the sea, where there is a hole in the ocean leading to the underworld. The water in that hole is called the Water of Life. Unfortunately, the authors did not have enough knowledge of geology, or the science of geology was not sufficiently advanced, for them to recognize the connection with volcanoes. In fact, much of *Hamlet's Mill* can be reinterpreted as describing volcanic and geological processes.

With our modern (around 2000 AD) knowledge of geology, or earth science, we can reinterpret many other classical myths, but as I said once before, this book is not meant to be an exhaustive survey. My purpose here is to show you that the myths are there, waiting to be correctly interpreted.

Let's return to Mott Greene to end this section:

> We should learn to accept more freely what the sources report to us, since it is largely due to their uncritical repetitions that much of the material of interest...has survived.
>
> None of the ruling theories of mythology—literary, functionalist, structuralist, Freudian, Jungian, ritualist—is of much help with this aspect of mythic texts, and all such theories hold the study of myth hostage to opposed camps of specialists engaged in a power struggle over the origins and nature of human thought in a way which can obscure the literal sense of the texts. If we cart off the freight of excessive theory and take the texts at their words, we can...perhaps come to a better understanding of the approach to natural phenomena that characterized Greek thought in the period down to 500 B.C.
>
> Anyone who studies this material has an obligation to gain some knowledge of geology, geomorphology, volcanology, and a host of allied sciences...if he or she wishes to have access to the text's message.
>
> Finally, no formalistic analysis of mythology, however polished, brilliant, time-tested, and attractive should ever be used to devalue the content of a myth until all possible avenues to a message of some sort being transmitted by that content have been exhausted. [130]

The Rise and Fall of Civilizations

There are many myths of destruction: the destruction of Osiris, the Flood of Noah, the battle of Rama and Ravana, the legends of Quetzalcoatl and Tezcatlipoca, etc. Here is a partial summary table of what we have discussed so far showing the geological identities:

Region	Magma-Lava	Volcanic Lightning
Egypt	Osiris	Seth
Greece	Titans	Zeus
India	Ravana, Vritra	Rama, Indra
Maya	Quetzalcoatl	Tezcatlipoca
China	P'an Ku	Shu-hu
Norse	Midgard Serpent	Thor
Rome	Phaethon	Jupiter

Even the Oedipal myth, where Oedipus kills his father and marries his mother, may have its origins in a volcano that explodes (the father), and then grows back anew (the son).

The new volcano appears to create life: the lava coming out of the cone reminded early humans of sperm and the merging of this sperm with Mother Earth appears to create new life. (However, we now know that the seeds are brought by flying birds or drift there on the wind or ocean.)

Some of these myths may refer to one early incident (at Krakatau, Thera or elsewhere), or many repeated incidents, or many separate but now blended incidents. This is not entirely clear. However, certainly early humans, living in Africa's Great Rift Valley, observed the volcanoes and codified this knowledge into stories. In addition, there may have been minor exchanges between the various cultures by sea and/or land.

Do your own investigation. Get a geological text and read the ancient myths. Look for words like "fire," "light," "creation" (such as a mound rising from the sea), "explosions," "thunder," "serpents," "underworlds," "flying," etc. Beware of translation errors. For example, flowing *rivers* of lava may be translated as "water" or "liquid." The word "flood" may refer to a flood of *liquid lava* rather than a flood of water. Finally, later renditions of the myth are often made into more human-like stories than the earlier ones.

To the early humans it seemed like both the Sun and the fire under the ground (magma) were eternal. They developed a Grand Unification Theory, such as "Fire-Earth-Water-Air" or even more condensed: *all things come from fire* (which may have been the beginning of monotheism). However, they eventually found that this didn't predict well enough, so they searched more, and this was the beginning of alchemy, which was not completely satisfactory either, and so then they developed chemistry, and the search continues for an even more comprehensive and accurate theories.

Certain religions try to slow or halt the recycling process by modern mummification and burial. They think this will allow the person to rise up again at the Judgment Day. However, the Judgment Day is really a volcanic explosion followed by a volcanic resurrection. It is said that Judgment Day will be accompanied by a "host of angels," which are, as we said, merely the lava bombs.

Recently, attention has been given to the effects of planetary impacts, thanks largely due to the theory that a comet or asteroid impacted the Earth, eventually resulting in the demise of the dinosaurs and the rise of the mammals. Also, the Jupiter impacts of comet Shoemaker-Levy 9, in July 1994, increased concern for this threat.

As a result, NASA is searching for Near-Earth Objects (NEOs) and cataloging their orbits.[131] A conference of 77 scientists from the US, Europe, and Japan in 2002 recommended, among other things, that (my emphasis):

- the future collision of an asteroid or cometary nucleus with the Earth with catastrophic effects is, without intervention, *inevitable*.
- numerous space missions will be required to acquire a relevant and adequate basis of knowledge on which to base the future development of a reliable collision mitigation system.
- estimates of the time necessary to acquire a relevant and adequate basis of knowledge on which to base the future development of a reliable collision mitigation system is measured in decades.

We recommend that government and international policy makers act now to formulate and publish an agreed upon chain of responsibility for action in the event that an Earth-threatening object is discovered.[132]

Not very encouraging, but yet it is a beginning. In addition, the B612 Foundation has as it goal "to significantly alter the orbit of an asteroid in a controlled manner by 2015." If they can demonstrate this, then it may be possible to deflect an incoming asteroid or comet just enough so that it misses Earth. In other words, if we act now, we may prevent a very large catastrophe.

A similar, also inevitable, catastrophe is brewing from volcanoes. When the huge magma chamber beneath Yellowstone Park eventually explodes, as it will do, that will be a "Judgment Day." Will we be prepared?

The officials of the Caribbean island of Martinique issued a report to the inhabitants of St. Pierre in 1902, just before the eruption of Pelée.

The report stated that "there is nothing in the activity of Mt. Pelée that warrants a departure from St. Pierre." It concluded that "the safety of St. Pierre is completely assured." The report eased the public's fears, and gave hope to city officials who were particularly anxious that voters remain in the city to cast their ballots for an election that was to be held on May 11.[133]

Of the 28,000 inhabitants of the city on the day of the eruption and pyroclastic flow (superheated toxic gases moving at hurricane force speeds), only two survived. In that eruption, there was no Noah who listened to nature (God), and took people and animals to safety. In fact, "Governor Mouttet [sent] in troops to patrol the road to Fort-de-France, with orders to turn back refugees who were trying to leave."[134] Those in power told people not to worry.

Midway across the island of Java sits the city of Yogyakarta. I visited it in 1997. The huge Prambanan Temples sit about 20 kilometers east of Yogyakarta. These temples were constructed in the 9th century by the Hindu dynasty. At the Prambanan Temples carved monsters flow out of rock stairways like lava flowing down a mountain.

Not far away is the Buddhist temple of Borobudur. It is the largest single Buddhist temple in the world. The circular cone shape reminds one of a mountain. It is said to represent a "holy mountain."

I have no doubt that both these temples were inspired by the large volcano, Merapi, simmering in the background, which can be seen on a clear day. The landscape around both temples is filled with rubble from buildings destroyed during the 1006 eruption of Merapi.[135] Says geologist Dorothy Vitaliano,

In the inscription telling of the destruction of Old Mataram it is hard to sort fact from fiction, but the volcanological record is clear. It shows that the old cone of Merapi collapsed in a cataclysmic fissure eruption which spread a thick blanket of ash over central Java, undoubtedly destroying its fertility for many decades and completely disrupting the drainage pattern.[136]

David Keys, like myself, is a dot-connector. In his interesting book, *Catastrophe*, he examines historical data regarding the period of about 535 AD: the plague, climate data from ice cores, climate data from historical references, the barbarian invasions of Rome, the Roman collapse, the rise of Islam, and changes in Western Europe, the Orient, and the Americas. He provides voluminous evidence that a climatic catastrophe occurred in this period, which resulted in the complete restructuring of the geopolitical face of the globe. His book is one of a few which connects earth science to its climatic and political consequences.

In brief, he suggests that volcano Krakatau violently erupted in 535 AD, and that this explosion caused particulates to be suspended in the air which blocked out solar radiation and triggered colder weather and crop failure. This colder weather also resulted in an increase in the rodent population in central East Africa. The expanding rodent population carried the plague virus to the Mediterranean and Europe by way of trade. *He suggests that this caused the collapse of the Roman Empire and the resulting restructuring of Europe.* He also suggests that this pattern of weather change resulted in similar catastrophic changes throughout the world leading to rise and fall of various empires, resulting in the political structure we have today.

According to Keys, there are several possible catastrophic mega-explosions that could occur in the future.

1) Yellowstone National Park, United States. This is a huge magma chamber. It erupted 2 million years ago, 1.3 million years ago, and 630,000 years ago. If this pattern continues then we are due for another eruption.

2) Long Valley/Mammoth Lakes, California, United States. This has become "progressively less stable" over the last 20 years. Last major eruption 700,000 years ago.

3) Naples, Italy. Another vast caldera that is becoming increasing restless. It had a mega eruption 37,000 years ago.

4) Rabaul, Papua, New Guinea. Major eruptions 1250 and 3500 years ago.

I would add to this 5) Merapi on Java, and several other potential huge eruptions in 6) Alaska and 7) Mexico.

Keys says our current political and scientific systems are unprepared to deal with them. "If any one of them was to explode, world climate would be plunged into chaos, precisely as it was in the 6th century...[it] would destabilize the economic and geopolitical status quo, leading to a second resynchronization of history." He continues,

> A major caldera eruption could quite easily disrupt climate to such an extent that hundreds of millions of people would die...political administration would rapidly disintegrate in many areas. Banditry would increase, huge refugee flows would develop, epidemics would break out, and the medical infrastructure would be totally overwhelmed. Cholera, measles, typhus, and dysentery epidemics would occur on a massive scale...the bubonic plague could again devastate substantial areas.[137]

Of course, geological activity such as the shifting of tectonic plates beneath the ocean floor can create an underwater earthquake and a resulting tsunami. Here is a diagram from Simpkin and Fiske (1983) showing the geological fault line that is bending Sumatra. The elbow of the bend is at Krakatau. This geologically active area is perhaps responsible for the periodic explosions and resurrections of Krakatau and the underwater earthquake-generated tsunamis. Add to this the periodic explosion and resurrection of Thera in the

Mediterranean, and one can see why the ancients were preoccupied with floods, judgement days, resurrection, and the building of great pyramids to symbolize these activities.

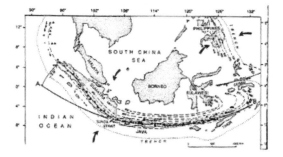

Can preventive measures do any good? Can scientists somehow devise a method of reducing the particulate matter after a mega-eruption? Can they somehow collect the particles or induce them to fall sooner to the ground? Will a mega-eruption somehow prevent global warming? Are we going to have to have another mega-eruption before we take any preventive measures?[138] Does the Earth need these eruptions to be "alive," unlike the mostly dead planet, Mars. These are some important questions that need to be answered.

6 ☼

The Chemistry of the Soul

... atmospheric air is not an element, that is, a simple body, but a mixture of several gases. Approximately a quarter of atmospheric air is composed by...eminently breathable air and three-quarters, of noxious and harmful air.

Anton Von Lavoisier (1743-1794)

A modern biology student knows things about biology that Darwin didn't know; a modern mathematics student knows things about mathematics that Archimedes didn't know; a modern physicist knows things about physics that Newton didn't know; a modern astronomer knows things about the stars that Kepler didn't know. Likewise, when you finish reading this part of the book, you will know things about the "soul" and "spirit" that all the great religious leaders of the past didn't know.[139]

In this chapter, using modern science, I explain the origin of the human "spirit" and human "soul." I will use a tool that Albert Einstein used. He would imagine illustrative scenarios involving the speed of light that he called "thought experiments." Using a "thought experiment," we will first examine the spirit and then the soul.

Background

Past theories of the soul include those of Plato, who wondered (incorrectly) if the soul made the Sun move. Aristotle (more correctly) thought that the soul gives life to all living things.

Edward B. Tylor, in *Primitive Culture*, and later, James Frazer, in *The Golden Bough* discuss the origin of the soul. I will concern myself here with a brief discussion of Tylor's work.

Tylor is often called the "father of anthropology." Tylor assumed that ancient humans used observation and deduction to develop their ideas of the soul and spirit.

The shadowy forms of men and women do appear to others, when the men and women themselves are at a distance, and after they are dead. We call these apparitions dreams or phantasms ...[140]

Tylor stated that the minimum definition of religion was belief in spiritual beings or "spiritualism." However, because the word "spiritualism" was associated with a popular cult at the time, he chose the word "animism." He believed that "spiritualism" or "animism" was found in all primitive cultures and he presented an impressive array of evidence to support that fact, drawing on the wealth of knowledge available to him from all parts of the globe.

Tylor thought that if ancient people saw a dead person in their sleep, or had a ghostly hallucination of them after their death, that they believed the person was still somehow alive. I call this the Dream Theory of the soul. I believe this theory to be false, and I will show why in the next two chapters.

Steven J. Gould wants to keep science and religion separate, saying science deals with the material world and religion the moral world.[141] This is an attempt to maintain the *status quo*. This approach serves to block any inquiry.

There are many more words written about the soul and the spirit. I do not wish to discuss all of them here. The reader is undoubtedly familiar with his or her own cultural paradigm regarding these things, and that is all that is really required, so let us press forward.

The Human Spirit: Blood and Oxygen?

Since we are discussing the spirit, lets first look at some definitions of it:

spirit: ME < L *spritus* a breathing[142]
spirit: the vital principal in humans, animating the body.
spirit: the incorporeal part of humans.

spirit: a divine, inspiring, or animating being or influence. [143]

Note the similarity to the definitions of blood:

· blood: the vital principal; life.
· blood: a person or group regarded as a source of energy, vitality or vigor.

Homo erectus differentiated or evolved somewhere around 2,000,000 years ago, possibly in Africa. We know that by 1.8 million years ago he/she was spread throughout much of Africa and Asia. Then around 100,000 years ago *Homo sapiens* appeared, possibly in Africa or in multiple locations. This is a gross oversimplification of the evolutionary "tree" and the evolutionary issues, but will do for our purposes here.

During these last two million years, the small hominid tribes gathered food, hunted when they could, fished and scavenged. They began to communicate with speech, at first using gestures, grunts and noises to represent various things, events and ideas. According to the current best estimates of archeologists, humans began to bury things with their dead sometime within 350,000 to 60,000 years ago. [144] Later, they buried their dead with human made items (tools, pots, ornaments, etc.). They apparently expected the dead person to live again, and have use for these artifacts. This behavior implies that ancient people had some idea of a "soul" or "afterlife."

The older people of this time probably were cared for, as they had developed wisdom of the surrounding environment. They knew which fruits, nuts, berries and mushrooms were safe to eat, etc. This was a primitive science.

These early humans (*Homo sapiens*) had a similar mental capacity that we have today—a similar high horsepower brain. They would want to know what motivates man and woman. What gives him or her life? What is life?

Let us look at the world from their eyes. Let us imagine ourselves in Africa around 100,000 years ago ...

When another human was wounded (perhaps they were gored by the horn of an angry rhino, perhaps pierced by a spear), they would see the body give off the red liquid. They would notice that when the person lost a certain amount of the red liquid, they would weaken. They would also notice that when the wounded person lost too much of the liquid, they would die.

For example, let us imagine two friends: Ayo and Obi. Let us imagine that while you are out hunting one day Obi is seriously wounded and the red liquid slowly drains out of him. As it does, Ayo sees him become increasingly lifeless, and less and less like the old Obi. He happens to be lying on a rocky mesa and the red liquid pools. Obi is now completely motionless. Obi has been a companion to Ayo for many years, and out of grief and shock, Ayo does not leave just yet. Ayo finds it hard to even imagine life without Obi by his side.

Ayo stares at the red liquid that has poured out of Obi onto the rocky ledge. Over the next few hours, *it slowly disappears into the air*, leaving behind only a red stain. Later that day Ayo starts to trudge slowly back to the base camp. Ayo has seen this sort of thing before in others. Ayo also has butchered many small animals. But never has a loss like this occurred to him from such a close friend.

Ayo has thought about this before, and now after some additional thought (and with help from the elders of the tribe), Ayo concludes that *that-which-makes-one-move* left Obi's body as red-liquid. Then, the *that-which-makes-one-move* left the red-liquid and went into the air. Obi's *that-which-makes-one-move* now exists for Ayo as an invisible entity in the air, a "disembodied spirit."

Thus, in Ayo's proto-science-religion, he puts together the picture (which was correct) that this red liquid was necessary for life. Ayo gives it a name, perhaps simply the *red-life-liquid,* and teaches its power to his children, eventually along with methods to stop the flow of blood during an injury.

Ayo has seen water mysteriously disappear into the air. He has seen heated water on a cold morning form a white mist that rises into the air and disappears. He does not know about "evaporation." He only knows that the *red-life-liquid,* that allows him to run, jump and procreate, can disappear into thin air like water ...

He deduces (correctly) that there is *something mysterious in the air* that gives animals life. He perhaps names it *invisible-and-formless-life-giver-in-the-air.* He also deduces (incorrectly, possibly out of grief) that this *invisible-and-formless-life-giver-in-the-air* is a self-organized personal unit. He calls it Obi's *invisible-and-formless-life-giver-in-the-air.* Later, this is shortened to Obi's "spirit" (or any number of different names depending on the culture).

When a new baby is born, he concludes that its *invisible-and-formless-life-giver-in-the-air* enters the baby. But where does it come from? He concludes that it comes from an ancestor or some greater invisible life-giver. (Perhaps he calls it the *Great-Spirit-Maker,* or simply the *Great Spirit.*)

He has no reason to believe that the ancestors' spirits or the *Great-Spirit,* which lies above the earth, ends anywhere. He assumes that it continues on UP. He associates UP with heaven, and he assumes that the invisible-and-formless-life-giver-in-the-air continues on UP into the realm of the Sun and the Stars, and the Wandering Stars (planets).

Because this idea of the invisible "spirit" is so important I am going to repeat the story from Ayo's viewpoint:

My name is Ayo. I want to speak-gesture to you about what happened to me. Yesterday, Obi and I were hunting. He was cut big, hunting with me boar. Red-liquid flowed out of him and he became still.

He was lying on flat rock and red-liquid made pool. Obi now completely motionless. Obi has been friend to me for many years and I cannot leave him. I find it hard to think about life without him.

I stare at red-liquid that has poured out of him onto rocky ledge.

Next few hours, it slowly disappears into air, leaving behind only red stain. Later that day I start to walk very slowly back to our camp. I have seen this thing before in others. I have also butchered many small animals. But never has someone so close to me died.

I tell Old One of tribe. He is my mother's, mother's brother. He calls it "red-life-liquid."

He tells me that *that-which-makes-one-move* of Obi, left his body with red-liquid. Then, *that-which-makes-one-move* left red-liquid and went in air. Obi's *that-which-makes-one-move* now lives in air.

In my head, I see that *red-life-liquid* is necessary for life. I want to teach about it. The Old One taught me about it. Maybe I might have saved Obi if I had known more about it. How to stop it from flowing out. The Old One showed me how to press against the body, and where to press, and then it would stop.

I have seen water mysteriously disappear into air. I have seen heated water on cold morning form white mist that rises up into air and disappears. I only know that *red-life-liquid,* that allows me to run, jump and make sex, can disappear somehow into thin air like water.

I decide there is *something mysterious in air* that gives animals life. I ask Old One about this. He calls it *invisible-life-giver-in-air.* I see that *invisible-life-giver-in-air* is Obi. I call it Obi's *invisible-life-giver-in-air.*

I later shorten this to Obi's "ssppiihh."

When new baby is born its *invisible-life-giver-in-air* enters baby. But where does it come from? It comes from some greater invisible life-giver. Perhaps I can call it *Great-Ssppiihh-Maker.* Or simply *Great Spihrit.* I see that Great Spihrit contains Spihrit of all ancestors.

Great-Spihrit, which lies above ground, above earth, never ends anywhere. It goes up. Up is heaven, and invisible-life-giver-in-air goes up to Sun and Stars and Wandering Stars, where it is perfect and forever. I burn incense for ancestors. It smells good and keeps ancestors happy. I leave food for ancestors. I kill pig for them and burn it. Make them happy.

Today, we say that "oxygen-carbon combustion" is what makes the body move. The oxygen burns the carbon fuel.

We say that blood is composed mostly of water molecules (about 90%), which is made of hydrogen gas and oxygen gas. These water molecules (H_2O) are constantly bouncing and jostling against each other. The ones on the surface of a liquid bounce away from the remainder, into the air. This natural process, called evaporation, continues until there are no more water molecules left, or the air is saturated with them.

Today we know that the atmosphere does not continue on UP, but that it ends rather close to the Earth's surface, and that the vast majority of space is devoid of air and oxygen.

It is only in the last few centuries that our modern atomic theory (thanks to Dalton, Mendeleev, Rutherford, and many others) has developed sufficiently for us to understand this process in greater detail. The early humans did not know about what we call atoms, the cyclical array of elements (including hydrogen and oxygen), or molecules such as H_2O. They just saw *the red-life-liquid* disappear into thin air.

Today, we say that oxygen molecules in the air are taken into the blood stream at the lungs and are carried to the tissues. In our more accurate (but more complex model), there is not some organized unit (composed of oxygen molecules) that can be used by only one person. If you look at the chart below, you will see various labels by which the spirit might go depending on the period or your personal orientation.

prehistoric	ancient	modern	scientific
that-which-makes-one-move	spirit	life-force	oxygen

Eventually, each primitive culture developed some idea of the "spirit." This is often popularly stated as proof that the spirit exists, and probably derives from Tylor's work. "How else could all these people come up with the same idea?" is the thinking.

Given the great time span involved and the importance of the body's fuel, I suspect that each tribe of ancient humans, whether in Asia, Africa, Europe, or later North and South America, saw and observed the *obvious*: the *red-life-liquid* pouring out of a wounded human (or animal) and then disappearing into the air. Partially out of grief, partially out of logical deduction, they invented the idea of a disembodied spirit. They passed this information on to the next generation orally. Eventually, some of them would find a way to write their findings in a primitive picture language, which may have become the first written language

The Human Soul: Oxygen?

Like we did with the spirit, let us first look at some definitions of the soul:

- Soul: the principal of life, feeling, thought, and action in humans, regarded as a distinct entity separate from the body, and commonly held to be separable in existence from the body.
- Soul: the animating principle; the essential element or part of something.

Note the similarities to breath:

- Breathe: to live; to exist.
- Breath: life, vitality.

Now, imagine yourself again observing fellow humans from the eyes of ancient Ayo. Besides the *red-life-liquid* that sustained and animated humans, what other most obvious sustaining factor would you see?

You would observe that living people take in and give off something in the air. You would observe that dead people *do not* take in and give off something. And you might see a person prevented from getting this something from the air by covering the mouth, by being underwater, by choking, by strangulation, by blocking the wind pipe, by being surrounded by too much smoke, etc. You would deduce (correctly) that this something, whatever it is, is also vital for life. You might have given it a name such as the *life-giver-in-the-air*. You would have communicated orally to your children about this something in the air that gave life to all animals.

Perhaps you would have thought, "That which gives life and motion to us is inside us, and all around us. When we die, that something must be outside us. That something (from the ancestors or the *Great Soul-Maker* outside of us) must then go into a baby to give life and motion to it. That *something* then must be always alive, always around us and never-ending."

Most, if not all, primitive cultures around the world would observe this process and develop the idea of an immortal "soul." Of course, this is not evidence that an immortal disembodied soul exists, but rather evidence of the observational and deductive power of *Homo sapiens* and perhaps even *Homo erectus*.

As with the spirit, the ancient people (incorrectly) anthropomorphized (made-human) this soul. As with the spirit, the

89

soul became a personal unit.

Let us now return to our world and chemistry.[145]

In 1783, the brilliant Frenchman and natural philosopher, Antoine Lavoisier showed through weighing that a substance, which he called "oxygen," was necessary to the burning process, and that oxygen combines with the substance burned. He showed that the older phlogiston theory was wrong. Lavoisier was also the first to do modern experimental work on animal respiration.

He was beheaded during the French revolution. When he pleaded with the judge for a few days to write up the results of his experiments the judge said, "The Republic has no need for savants."[146] Said a friend, "It took but a moment to cut off that head which a hundred years would be unable to replace."[147]

Today, in the atomic theory, we say that of the 118 or so chemical elements discovered thus far, oxygen is element number 8. We now say that by using the energy of the Sun (photosynthesis), plants build up large carbon chains. Oxygen enters our bodies through the lungs. Red blood cells "carry" this oxygen to the cells, where it "burns" (breaks apart) these large chains of carbon, releasing this stored solar energy for use by the body. In the process, the oxygen combines with the carbon to form carbon dioxide (CO_2), which is then expelled by the lungs.

The "burning" is similar to the burning of petroleum in your car, the burning of wood, and even the rusting of metals. This expelled CO_2 might then get taken up by a plant, which uses the C, carbon, and energy of the Sun (photosynthesis), to start the cycle again. In short, in our new model, we take in oxygen and give off CO_2. Plants take in CO_2 and give off oxygen. It is a marvelous cycle.

So, it wasn't until Lavoisier that we began to fully understand the nature of fire. For millennia, the "soul" was just the "invisible-life-giver-in-the-air" or what we now call "oxygen."

Let's look at some definitions of "oxygen" and "respiration."

- oxygen: A gaseous element that constitutes 21 percent of the atmosphere by volume, is essential for plant and animal respiration.
- respiration: breathing; the sum total of physical and chemical processes in an organism by which oxygen is conveyed to tissues and cells, and the oxidation products, carbon dioxide and water are given off.

By understanding these definitions we can in one sense see what the "soul" is, and what it is doing, but on a much more detailed level than the ancients.

Cremations are done in the range of 760-1150 C.[148] Some forest fires reach temperatures of 800 C. Early humans may have first seen an accidental cremation in a forest fire. Of course, they saw that when a body burned that it completely disappeared except for bone fragments and ashes. All that was left was about 5% of the original. (Later, of course, they began to purposely cremate.)

They assumed that even the person's personality and desire was made of "soul." Of course, today we know that these are a result of the interaction of genes and the environment of the person.

Why the Popularity of the Spirit and Soul?

We seem to understand what is meant when someone says that they have a "soul" or "spirit." People say, "I am a spiritual being." They seem to find it helpful to say this. Why?

Element	% in living things
Oxygen	65%
Carbon	19%
Hydrogen	9%
Others	4%
Nitrogen	3%

If we try to translate this statement into the scientific model it would read, "I am, on the inside, circulating blood, which is 90% liquid water, which carries oxygen and fuel to the body."

In fact, from the chart we see that a remarkable 74 percent of living things are composed of oxygen and hydrogen gas. Sixty-five percent is just oxygen. One might wonder why we just don't float away. The answer is that oxygen has weight. A 150-pound person is 97.5 pounds of oxygen! The blanket of air surrounding the Earth, as well as the oxygen inside you, is held there by gravity. So on the one hand you weigh much less than if you were all iron (about 1350 pounds), like a statue, but you weigh much more than if you were all hydrogen (in which case you would float away). We are between these two.

When one is under too much stress, or working in an unnatural way (for example, staring at a computer screen for hours each day, instead of running, walking, jumping, or scanning the horizon for potential food, predators, prey and mates) certain muscles contract (depending on the circumstances and person) and the blood does not flow well (circulate) into that particular area of the body, especially to the smaller tubes called capillaries. Numbness and disease can result.

When one sleeps, meditates, or sits quietly in a church or temple, the muscles have a chance to relax again, and the blood can reach into the previously blocked areas. One "feels better" as the normal, healthy circulation returns. Healing can occur.

In a like manner, we make comments about our "soul." We say, "A drive in the country is good for my soul." Scientific translation: "On a drive in the country, I get away from the poisonous fumes (smog) of the city, and I can breathe the oxygen given off by the abundant greenery of the country. I experience the natural green environment in which my genes evolved. I am close to the carbon-oxygen cycle."

God is in the Air?

We often hear, "God is everywhere in the air." By seeing the world from ancient eyes, we can easily see how they could develop this idea of "God" from, or alongside of, their invisible "soul" and "spirit." Earlier, we talked about the Soul-Maker and the Spirit-Maker. These, of course, would eventually have been simplified into the word "God." Alternatively, in some traditions they were made into a "reincarnation" philosophy.

So there was a difference between how different parts of the world modeled this. Either, 1) the soul comes from "God" or 2) the soul is recycled. For example, in India, there would be the recycling of souls.

Through accidental or purposeful burning of animal bodies (including human bodies) the ancient humans probably learned that these bodies, besides containing the red-life-liquid, are composed of a few ashes, and what? Again, they probably assumed it was the *invisible-and-formless-life-giver-in-the-air*.

This was a very important observation. This strengthened the belief that, "the soul (or spirit) resides in the body." Today, of course, we say that the body is mostly composed of water (which would turn into water *vapor* upon burning) as well as carbohydrates that would be turned into carbon dioxide gas (CO_2), hydrogen gas, oxygen gas, and the few remaining ashes of carbon.

So, in a sense they were right. The body is about 65%

oxygen. The soul (as oxygen) does reside in the body. They did not know about oxygen though, and to say that, "the soul resides in the body" was their way of modeling the same event.

With the process of cremation (burning the body) they tried to help return the "soul" or "spirit" to the air or heaven where it could join the other ancestors, be recycled or rejoin the Great Spirit.

As with the "spirit" and the "soul," the "Great Spirit," or "God," turns out to be something material in the scientific model: oxygen, water vapor and perhaps some other gaseous elements.

Thus, although the early humans saw the same basic element (oxygen) that inspired them to generate the ideas "God," "soul," "spirit," there were many different twists and turns after this, which led to some of the differences that we see in religions today.

I recently found a passage in Freud's *Moses and Monotheism*, written over 60 years ago, that discusses breath and the soul.

Man found that he was faced with the acceptance of 'spiritual' forces —that is to say, such forces as cannot be apprehended by sight, and yet have undoubted, even extremely strong effects. If we trust to language, it was the movement of air that provided the image of spirituality, since the spirit borrows its name from the breath of wind (animus, spiritus, Hebrew ruach = smoke). The idea of soul was thus born as the spiritual principle in the individual. Observation found the breath of air again in the human breath, which ceases with death; even today we talk of a dying man breathing his last. Now the realm of the spirits had opened for man, and he was ready to endow everything in nature with the soul he had discovered in himself. The whole world became animated, and science, coming so much later, had enough to do in disestablishing the former state of affairs and has not yet finished the task.[149]

He was right. Science has not yet finished the task.

7 ☼

The Oxygen Gods

> *... the enduring paradox of religion is that so much of it is demonstrably false yet it remains a driving force in all societies ... Man would rather believe than know ... Since [1900] ... social scientists have sought the psychological Rosetta stone that might clarify the deeper truths of religious reasoning.*[150]
>
> E. O. Wilson

I predicted that the other myths of the world would have also generated models of oxygen that would be embedded in their most sacred texts. Let us see if that prediction is correct. Let's see if we can find part of that Rosetta stone that E. O. Wilson talks about in the above quote.

China and Asia

Chi or Qi, which is called the "vital energy" in the ancient Chinese teachings, means "breath"! "Tai chi," the slow moving exercise, means, "highest breathing," and "qi gong" literally means "skill at breathing." Some current publications translate "qi" as "energy" or "vital energy" or "universal energy" or "vital energy that circulates round the body in currents."[151] Unfortunately, people think that they are getting some kind of special energy, not just oxygen.

In Buddhism *nirvana* is "the ineffable ultimate in which one has attained disinterested wisdom and compassion. A transcendent state in which there is neither suffering nor desire, no sense of self, and the subject is released from the effects of karma. It represents the final goal in Buddhism. A state of perfect happiness."[152]

Let us look further into the etymology of the Indian word "nirvana." Here are three sources:

1) from Sanskrit, nirva- be extinguished + nis- out + va- to blow.[153]

2) from Sanskrit, "extinction, disappearance" (of the individual soul into the universal), literally "to blow out, a blowing out" ("not transitively, but as a fire ceases to draw)" A literal Latinization would be de-spiration), from nis-, nir- "out" + va "to blow."[154]

3) nirvana means liberation. Its derivation is from the prefix nir, which means 'nothing, devoid of, free', and vana, which means 'arrow', 'waves', and 'breath'.[155] Literally, it means "no-breath."

Again we see the early fascination with breath and the invisible-and-formless-life-giver-in-the-air. (We can see nirvana in the modern day vent, wind and windows.) Nirvana appears to be describing the situation wherein life ends and the person ceases to take in oxygen. Originally, it seems to have meant that when a person dies they blow out their last breath and their flame is extinguished. The candle flame is a metaphor Buddha used, and this is correct to some degree in our modern scientific model: as the organism ceases to be able to use oxygen to burn carbon-molecular fuel, it dies.

Continuing with our analysis, it appears early humans noticed that something in the air gave motion, energy and desire to humans. (Now we know that DNA and the environment interact to invoke desire.) They felt that when a person died, that person would, as I said, "become one" with the grand spirit or soul surrounding them and they would attain "disinterested wisdom and compassion." The oxygen represented compassion, as it surrounded them, and seemed eternal and unconditionally loving. However, it also seemed disinterested (it was, after all, just matter-energy).

So, the rather surprising fact is "nirvana" probably was just a way to express what we call "death." It was a proto-scientific word representing a proto-scientific idea attempting to describe (or match) the surrounding world. It has been grossly misunderstood (as have most religious terms), as referring to something "beyond the physical" or "metaphysical."

In addition, we see here an action that is visible in many cultures: people becoming spiritual in their older years. This inevitably happens whether they do it consciously or not. We may all end up as spirit-atoms recycled into the biosphere no matter what.[156]

We see "spirit" also expressed throughout the *Tao Teh Ching*. I believe the Tao was originally what we call oxygen. Here are some excerpts from the ancient text.[157] Notice the similarities.

> It is the nature of the Tao,
> that even though used continuously,
> it is replenished naturally,
> never being emptied,
> and never being over-filled,
> as is a goblet
> which spills its contents
> upon the ground.
> The Tao therefore cannot be said
> to waste its charge,
> but constantly remains
> a source of nourishment ...
>
> ... The Tao ... has no form,
> it is neither bright in rising,
> nor dark in sinking,
> cannot be grasped, and makes no sound ...
> ... The creative principle unifies
> the inner and external worlds.
> It does not depend on time or space,
> is ever still and yet in motion;
> thereby it creates all things,
> and is therefore called
> 'the creative and the absolute';
> its ebb and its flow extend to infinity ...
> ... The Tao creates, not claiming credit,
> and guides without interfering.

Here us another selection from the Sanderson Beck translation[158]:

> The Way produces all things.
> Power nourishes them.
> Matter gives them physical form.
> Environment shapes their abilities.

Therefore all things respect the Way and honor
power.
The Way is respected, and power is honored
without anyone's order and always naturally.

Therefore the Way produces all things,
and power nourishes them,
caring for them and developing them,
sheltering them and comforting them,
nurturing them and protecting them,
producing them but not possessing them,
helping them but not obligating them,
guiding them but not controlling them.
This is mystical power.

It is interesting that the earliest mention of gunpowder is in a
Taoist book from the Ninth Century![159] *The Classified Essentials of
the Mysterious Tao of the True Origin of Things* lists thirty-five
"wrong or dangerous" formulations, including one formulation that
says never to mix sulfur, arsenic disulfide, saltpeter (potassium
nitrate) and honey, which are the essential ingredients of the
explosive fire-powder.[160] Understanding oxygen would be important
to understanding fire-powder. This shows that the Tao was more than
an abstract metaphysical teaching, but rather another early attempt to
understand the natural world and what we call oxygen.

Of course, early humans thought that, "oxygen" extended out
into space. They had no way of going there as we do. In their limited
perspective, they thought the "spirit" or "oxygen" was infinite. If you
read the *Tao The Ching* (from the Oxygen = Tao perspective), you
will see that it urges us to act as what we call "oxygen" acts. Oxygen
nourishes, yet it is dispassionate. It is not violent, yet it survives
eternally (or at least for a very long time).

Is it right to try to model behavior on the behavior of oxygen?
Should we be nourishing, nonviolent, yielding yet surviving? Those
are questions beyond the scope of this book. However, we'll see other
cultures also suggesting this.

In Japan, there is a healing system known as Reiki, which
may have originated in Tibet. Here are two definitions:

The word Reiki comes from two Japanese words - Rei and Ki, meaning
universal life energy.[161]

Reiki (pronounced ray-key) is a Japanese word representing universal life
energy, the energy that is all around us. It is derived from rei, meaning "free
passage" or "transcendental spirit" and ki, meaning "vital life force energy" or

"universal life energy".[162]

It doesn't take a rocket scientist to see that Reiki probably referred to oxygen. It may have meant something like the "free passage of oxygen." Unfortunately, nowadays it has come to have an esoteric, "metaphysical" meaning, rather than the simple, original, physical, and quite practical, meaning.

India

When I studied Hinduism at the Air Force Academy in 1971, I learned the key ideas of "Atman," "Brahman" and "Maya."

Atman means "breath." Atman is the "soul within" and Brahman is the "soul outside."

In Hinduism, nirvana is said to be, "salvation through the union of Atman with Brahma." The union of the Atman (oxygen in the body) with the Brahman (oxygen outside of the body) is of course what we do while breathing and more completely at death by cremation (a common practice in India).

Yoga puts great emphasis on breathing as a way to connect with God, primarily through meditation and awareness. In our modern scientific terminology, Atman is the oxygen within the body, and Brahman is the oxygen outside the body. By focusing on the breath, one focuses on the nourishment from oxygen and one's connection with the outside.

In the ancient Indian text, *Mahabharata*, we find another word for oxygen: Prana. Here is an excerpt: "Through the breath called Prana a living creature is enabled to move." Also, "That Prana is the living creature, the universal soul, the eternal Being, and the Mind, Intellect and Consciousness of all living creatures, as also all the objects of the senses. Thus the living creature is, in every respect, caused by Prana to move about and exert."[163]

Here a quote from Swami Vivekananda (1863-1902).

It is the Prana that is manifesting as motion; it is the Prana that is manifesting as gravitation, as magnetism. It is the Prana that is manifesting as the actions of the body, as the nerve currents, as thought force. From thought, down to the lowest physical force, everything is but the manifestation of Prana. The sum total of all force in the universe, mental or physical when resolved back to its original state, is called Prana.[164]

We can see how he diverges from the correct "oxygen-seeking" attempts of the ancients. *This is a common fallacy: to interpret the ancient name for what we now call "oxygen," as some*

99

sort of "universal energy." Certainly, what we now call oxygen seemed to the ancients to be universal. Their universe was limited however to the surface of the earth. They had not yet performed experiments in the laboratory; they had not yet traveled deep under the sea or into space. For them, "oxygen" was indeed the "universal energy."

In India, they allow the soul to be "free" by burning the person into ashes. There is a certain amount of truth to this as the person's 62.8% oxygen-soul is released upon burning into the atmosphere. However, the oxygen atoms do not stay together in an individual soul, but are spread in a trillion trillion different ways into the biosphere.

Here are some definitions of "Maya," another important concept in Hinduism:

Maya: the name for the doctrine of the unreality of matter ...[165]
Maya: the illusion of the reality of sensory experience and of the experienced qualities and attributes of oneself. [166]
Maya: the true nature of the cosmos we can see. In Sanskrit, the word means "illusion," but that does not just mean that it is imaginary. Instead, since it is what we can see, we must deal with it and live within it. [167]

Today we are likely to call *air* "matter," but back then, at the time of the early humans, *matter* was the hard, *rigid* thing, and *spirit* was the soft thing that you couldn't grasp with the hand like air.

With our model of the Oxygen-Soul, does "Maya" make some sense? Yes, it does. It is the reality that one can touch: matter. Not matter in the modern scientific sense, but matter in the sense of a rock as opposed to the air.

In other words, the early humans saw that when one is cremated that one becomes nothing but ashes and spirit-oxygen. Therefore, they were able to establish that the *rigid* things (wood, rocks, bodies, etc.) were mostly made of an invisible substance (which today we call "oxygen"). Also, the early alchemists, having seen volcanoes and gotten clues to the underlying nature of matter, were able to see that these hard things could be translated by fire into the air or spirit-oxygen. So, the Hindus were able to say that matter was an *illusion,* and they were somewhat correct in this.

Here are some excerpts on *maya.* [my comments will be in brackets]

Maya is the power that deludes ...
How is the delusion caused? It is caused through the senses. The

Bhagavad gita explains the process, 'By constantly thinking of the sense objects, a mortal being becomes attached to them. Attached thus he develops various desires, from which in turn ensues anger. From anger comes delusion, and from delusion arises confusion of memory. From confusion of memory arises loss of intelligence and when intelligence is lost the breath of life is also lost (2.60-63).'

Maya causes delusion in many ways. Under the influence of Maya an individual loses his intelligence and power of discretion. He forgets his true nature. He loses contact with the self within [oxygen] and believes that he is the ego with a body and a name. In that delusion, he assumes that he is doer of his actions, where as in truth he is just an instrument of God, who is the real doer. He develops attachment with worldly objects and wants to possess them. He strives for wrong objectives in the world, having lost his connection with the real self [oxygen] and having forgotten the true purpose of his existence...

One can overcome the power of maya, by developing detachment, by withdrawing the senses from sense objects, by surrendering to God and by performing desireless actions accepting God as the doer.

Does Hinduism consider the world in which we live as real or unreal? Hinduism considers the world in which we live as a projection of God and unreal. It is unreal not because it does not exist, but because it is unstable, impermanent, unreliable and illusory. It is unreal because it hides the Truth and shows us things that lead to our ignorance. It is unreal because it changes its colors every moment. What is now is not what is next...[168]

Notice the similarity to the teachings from China about the Tao. It appears that some early humans thought we should remember that we are mostly oxygen. If we forget it, we strive after material things, only to find later that we return (and much of the material things also) to being oxygen. They believed that to be more balanced and aware, we should remember we are filled with God-Oxygen. They believed we should remember God-Oxygen is the eternal reality and those other things, including us, are transitory.

Rigid bodies deteriorate while biospheric oxygen seems eternal. To the early Hindus the "sense objects" would not include the air and the oxygen in it. By focusing on air or oxygen they felt they were getting closer to reality.

Greece

The word "psych" comes from the Greek word "psyche," which originally meant "breath," "spirit," or "soul." The word sounds like the breath hissing out of the mouth when you say it. Try saying it. Try saying it with the original "p." Ppppssssyyychh. It was probably named because the word sounds like the breath.

In Plato we read: "And in the centre [of the body] he put the soul, which he diffused throughout the body, making it also to be the exterior environment of it."[169] Also in Plato, we read about Socrates in his last hours. Notice the similarity to the *Tao Teh Ching* and other stories [my emphasis]:

... while we are in the body, and while *the soul is mingled with this mass of evil*, our desire will not be satisfied, and our desire is of the truth. For the body is a source of endless trouble to us by reason of the mere requirement of food; and also is liable to diseases which overtake and impede us in the search after truth: and by filling us so full of loves, and lusts, and fears, and fancies, and idols, and every sort of folly, prevents our ever having, as people say, so much as a thought. For whence come wars, and fightings, and factions? whence but from the body and the lusts of the body? ... and all experience shows that *if we would have pure knowledge of anything we must be quit of the body, and the soul in herself must behold all things in themselves*: then I suppose that we shall attain that which we desire, and of which we say that we are lovers, and that is wisdom, not while we live, but after death, as the argument shows; *for if while in company with the body the soul cannot have pure knowledge,* one of two things seems to follow--either knowledge is not to be attained at all, or, if at all, *after death. For then, and not till then, the soul will be in herself alone and without the body.* In this present life, I reckon that we make the nearest approach to knowledge when we have the least possible concern or interest in the body, and are not saturated with the bodily nature, but remain pure until the hour when God himself is pleased to release us. *And then the foolishness of the body will be cleared away and we shall be pure and hold converse with other pure souls, and know of ourselves the clear light everywhere; and this is surely the light of truth.*[170]

Of course he was speaking from a limited scientific perspective. The point is that the similarity to the Tao, etc., is not proof of the existence of the soul, but proof of the observational power of humans everywhere.

Ancient Egypt and the Ka

In the Nile River Valley hieroglyphs, we find the word "Ka," translated as "spirit." Let us explore their idea of the Ka, considering our recent propositions. Here are some definitions and comments. Note the similarities to our *red-life-liquid* that can become the *invisible-and-formless-life-giver-in-the-air*:

Ka: a spiritual entity, an aspect of the individual, believed to live within the body during life and to survive it after death. [171]
Ka: the vital energy that both sustains and creates life, depicted as a duplicate of the physical body. Funerary rites were spoken to the Ka of the deceased.[172]

The Oxygen Gods

R. T. Rundle Clark, a noted Egyptologist, said: "Everyone is a receiver of divine power and everyone is an individual, so each has his own Ka ... The individual Ka is a kind of spiritual double which determines the good or fortunate aspects of one's fate. Hence, the Egyptian's said, 'To your Ka!' where we would wish good health and prosperity ... The Ka's, generally, are the ancestors, and to beget a child is to forge a link with them."[173]

Note that Ka determines "fate" just as DNA from an ancestor (one's blood) can determine much of one's fate. Current estimates: personality and intelligence are about half due to heredity and half due to environment. Look at these definitions of blood.[174]

· blood: one of the four elemental body humors of medieval physiology, regarded as causing cheerfulness.
· blood: temperament; state of mind.
· blood: physical nature of human beings.
· blood: descent from a common ancestor; ancestry; lineage.

Now compare them to these quotes from the ancient hieroglyph texts:

If a great man is presiding over the meal
his humour will be according to his Ka ...[175]

For your son belongs to the generation of your Ka.[176]

Washed is thy Ka, sittith thy Ka, it eateth bread with thee unceasingly for ever. Thou art pure, thy Ka is pure, thy soul is pure, thy form is pure.[177]

The famous English Egyptologist, E.A. Wallis Budge, said: "The Ka could eat food, and it was necessary to provide food for it..." Here, I interpret the Ka to be a personal unit probably derived originally from blood (needing food) and then evaporated blood. Budge added, "This abstract personality could move freely from place to place, separating itself from, or uniting itself to, the body at will, and also enjoying a life with the Gods in heaven."[178]

The Ka was also connected with the red-life-liquid that nourishes the muscles: Griffith (quoted by Budge) said: "it [Ka] was from one point of view regarded as the source of muscular movement and power, as opposed to 'ba,' the will or the soul which set it in motion."[179]

Finally, a point that highlights the connection between blood and religion: the word, "bless," means to consecrate or to make sacred. It is originally related to the word "blood." "Bless" originally meant in Old English, "bledsian," or "to make sacred with blood."

Ancient Egypt and the Ba

About the Ba, E. A. Wallis Budge said:

a word that has been thought to mean something like 'sublime,' 'noble' and which has always hitherto been translated by 'soul' or 'heart-soul.' It was closely associated with the Ka ... and *it was one of the principles of life in man*. In its form it is depicted as a human-headed hawk, and in nature and substance it is stated to be exceedingly refined or ethereal. It revisited the body in the tomb and re-animated it, and it conversed with it; *it could take any shape that it pleased* ... [180] [my emphasis]

This certainly fits well with oxygen, which, as a gas has the "spontaneous tendency to become distributed uniformly throughout any container."[181] In fact, the Nile River Valley people represented the soul, or Ba, symbolically as a human-headed hawk, since a bird could also move through the air like oxygen. (See earlier image.)

This *invisible-and-formless-life-giver-in-the-air,* which they called the Ba, went in and then came out again. If one tried to keep it out, or tried to keep it in, one died. Ancient humans, in their scientific search, observed the *invisible-and-formless-life-giver-in-the-air*, and named it Ba. Thus "Ba" is just an early attempt to describe what we now call "oxygen."

The Mediterranean and the Judeo-Christian Cultures

Genesis 2:7 says, "... the Lord God formed the man from the dust of the ground and breathed into his nostrils the breath of life, and the man became a living being." This is, of course, a reference to the oxygen that animates us.

At an evangelical church I attended recently, people held up their arms stretched out to the ceiling as they were singing "Let Jesus into your heart." The arms were in the exact position to let in the maximum amount of oxygen into the lungs. No doubt, people get some health benefits from standing and singing in this position. So in churches nowadays, Jesus is linked not only to the volcanic resurrection but to oxygen as well.

Also, I have listened to a fire and brimstone (burn-stone) radio-evangelist preacher, and I realized that even in modern Christian lore, Satan is the hard matter (the physical plane of desire), while Jesus-God is the soft, flowing (non-rigid) oxygen. This is just as in the Maya-Self dichotomy expressed in Hinduism.

Thus, although some philosophies claim that the spirit is

separate from the body, it appears to be only partially true. In fact, some pilots claim to have had out-of-body experiences after being in a centrifuge. It appears that the nervous system has to *recalibrate* after being spun around, and the result is this out-of-body experience. Certain mental exercises may be able to also reproduce this "recalibration" out-of-body phenomenon.

This, of course, does not prove that the "soul" or "spirit" is separate from the body. When you spin your body around and then suddenly stop, the world seems to keep spinning. This is also an illusion, not the true state of affairs.

It appeared at this point in my investigation that mythology and religion could be reexamined, not only considering modern geology, but also considering the "soul" as "oxygen," and they would now make sense. That is what I attempted next, and the results were again astonishing.

8 ☼

The Worship of Oxygen

> *The Astonishing Hypothesis is that "you,"*
> *your joys and your sorrows, your memories*
> *and your ambitions, your sense of personal*
> *identity and free will, are in fact no more that*
> *the behavior of a vast assembly of nerve cells*
> *and their associated molecules.*[182]
>
> Francis Crick

Enlightenment

Using the "oxygen as soul" idea, I think we can better understand the meaning of "enlighten," or en-lighten, or to give spiritual light to. We know now that with every inhalation, oxygen is taken in, and, as I have said, this oxygen allows the burning of carbon molecules. (In other words, the oxygen allows a burning, which, of course, always gives off light and heat.) Those carbon molecules were formed earlier by the light and energy of the Sun (the Home Star) that bound together the carbon (from carbon dioxide in the air). The taking in of oxygen allows a burning or unbinding of the carbon and a release of the stored energy of the Home Star. You are literally being *enlightened* with every breath-oxygen-spirit you take!

Perhaps this is why some mystics would laugh at someone trying to achieve enlightenment. It happens all the time without doing anything at all! Also, seeking a "spiritual union with God" would appear to be just as foolish. It is happening all the time.

It is difficult to accept the fact that our cherished spirituality is nothing more than oxygen. We think: It can't be! Say it isn't so! We think: spirituality is *invisible*. But so is oxygen. We think: spirit is in everything: people, rocks, trees, etc. But oxygen is in all these things too. It may be that we are overvaluing spirituality or undervaluing oxygen. Perhaps we should write odes to oxygen.

Eternity

To the ancients it seemed like the air always had been here, and would always be here, so they called it *eternal*. The Spirit was to them *eternal*. We know now that oxygen, what the early humans called "spirit" or the "soul" is not eternal.[183]

For oxygen has not always been abundant in the Earth's 4.6-billion-year history. Geochemist Dick Holland of Harvard University writes, "Without the Great Oxidation Event [a dramatic rise of oxygen in Earth's atmosphere some 2.3 billion years ago], we would not be here. No dinosaurs, no fish, no snakes—just a lot of microorganisms."[184]

The exact mechanism of why oxygen became more abundant at this time, after two billion years, is still being debated.

For whatever reason, "oxygen was able to build up in the atmosphere, causing perhaps the most dramatic shift in the history of life on the planet. Before that happened, the amount of oxygen in Earth's atmosphere was about one ten-quadrillionth of the amount present today ..."[185]

Marsh and Crawford elaborate: At first the blue-green algae and bacteria existed. For 1.6 billion years they had a monopoly, "Then in a short time, a whole series of radical changes took place and the boundaries of life exploded outwards. One of these changes was the coming of oxygen."[186] Oxygen made possible the new, more complex cells and the air-breathing animals. "At about 500 million years ago, multicellular life explodes onto the scene."[187] The colonization of land and air required the energy of oxygen. Oxygen users can produce more energy per unit of time. Energy can be produced eight times more efficiently with oxygen than without.

Unfortunately, water contains very little oxygen available for use by animals. The land-water interface, on the other hand, contains higher concentrations of oxygen as do freshwater rivers that stream into the ocean. So life took advantage of the abundant oxygen at the interface and eventually the abundant oxygen of the land.

We now know that life existed for about 1.4 billion years before oxygen even became a major component of the air. Logically, if oxygen can rise it can also fall. There is a possibility we could have a runaway greenhouse effect (as on Venus), and once again there would be no oxygen to support our kind of life.

However, look at oxygen from an ancient perspective. To them, in their limited perspective, oxygen always was present. We run, work, play, and yet there is always plenty of air (or spirit) for us. It seems unlimited. To the ancients, oxygen seemed unlimited and hence they developed the idea of *unlimited love*. (Although the constant *shining of the sun* may have helped with this idea.)

At some point in the future, our Home Star will finish its life cycle. Scientists have studied the life cycles of stars and know them fairly well. Our Home Star is of the type that will eventually evaporate our oceans (in about another three billion years) and then (in about another four billion years) become a "red giant" and, eventually collapse to become what is called a "white dwarf."

Early humans, in their much more limited perspective, saw that the spirit-oxygen was there for them, no matter how many sins they had. They felt that the spirit-oxygen was *unconditionally nourishing* and so we have the beginning of the idea of *unconditional love*.[188]

Faith, Grace, Sacrifice

Before the agricultural revolution (ten thousand years ago), when we were still hunter-gatherers, ancient people saw the killing of animals, saw the blood flowing out as the animal died, saw the last gasping breath for oxygen (spirit).

Then someone figured out that certain foods, such as grain, could be stored for long periods, and were not toxic if they were then cooked. A complex system of labor division began for the first time—the class systems had begun, with rulers and priests and farmers and butchers and shoemakers, etc. The general population no longer saw volcanoes, birth and death. The ancient teachings did not make sense to these people. They began to question the teachings and were told *to have faith.*

Today, we know that we have been *selected* by nature because of certain genetic characteristics. The fact that we have been *selected* by nature, of course means that God's "grace" is certain. Those who were not selected would not feel that God had much grace, but then they are not around. So we see that God's grace is sort of built into the system. Huston Smith was somewhat right in his "perennial philosophy," a philosophy of optimism due to God's grace.

However, we do not know if our particular genes will be eliminated from the gene pool by various, sometimes violent, acts of nature. That is a reason to worry. Although we might take solace in the fact that identical genes exist in relatives that we have helped, and that our energy, as atoms, continues on in a new form.

In ancient times, sometimes a volcano would not explode for long periods of time. This was an example of the "freely given, unmerited favor and love of God," or *grace*. Grace is also defined as "the influence or spirit of God operating in humans to regenerate or strengthen them."[189] This sounds a lot like a definition of atmospheric oxygen. The fact that *Homo sapiens* has expanded to more than six billion people as of this writing is an example of God's grace. No matter how many wars or how much violence and suffering there appears to be, the fact is that from the big picture, God's grace, to humans at least, is quite evident.

The ancients thought that the Great Spirit, Souls and Spirits of the dead lived in the air. They would sometimes offer burnt offerings to them. A burning animal also would disappear into the air (like in a cremation), and so the ancient mind thought the animal had gone to the same place as their dead ancestors. They believed this burnt animal could feed their ancestors' spirits. This was known as a *sacrifice*. Burning (nice smelling) *incense* was thought to appease the spirits. (*Incense* is from the Latin "to set on fire.") In China (where I am currently), you can buy money (that is fake) and burn it so that your ancestors have use of it.

Altar, which is a mound or platform, probably is from the Latin adolere, "to ritually burn." An altar was where the sacrifices were made so the "spirit" of the sacrificed could join the "spirit" of the ancestor.

Burning was making something "holy" because it was putting it into the realm of the spirit-oxygen, uniting it again with the main constitute of the Earth's crust and all living things. When fire burns something, it disappears and the fire is said to "devour it," or eat it. By burning things (food, incense, animals) early humans also thought they were feeding their Gods. By feeding Them they hoped to bring favor on themselves. However, in the scientific model we say they were not really feeding Gods, but simply recycling atoms and molecules. They were chemically changing the elements from one form to another. Complex carbohydrates were breaking apart into CO_2 (gas), O_2, and H_2O (vapor).

The Grand Unification Theory of the Ancients

Sacrifice comes from the word sacri- (or holy) + facere (to make) or "to make holy." Holy derives from the word "whole." In the 1980s and 1990s much talk was given to the GUT, the Grand Unification Theory. As I said before, the ancients had their own attempts to unify nature's phenomena. Initially, someone may have used the word "whole." The Whole Theory. Now, it has become just "*holy*." GUT of today was the HOLY of yesterday. (Some scientists also pursued the GUT with religious ardor.)

However, the ancients did not know that the oxygen content became less as one went higher in the sky. They probably thought that the heavens also contained spirit-oxygen. (As I have said, try to see the world as they did.)

To them, the Spirit-Oxygen continued on until it reached the Moon and the planets and the stars. *Also, they thought (somewhat incorrectly) that the Fire-Magma-Light beneath the Earth and the Light from the heavens was the same Light, and in between was the Light of Lightning and the Spirit.* As heavenly bodies passed "below the horizon" into the underworld, they could renew their supply of food (magma, soma or ambrosia) and so continue to burn brightly when they "rose" the next morning. This was the ancient Grand Unified Theory or Theory of Everything. This was the Whole or Wholly or Holy. (Although to some, the invisible Spirit became the Whole or Holy Spirit. All things were seen to come from the Spirit, as when lightning comes out of the air.)

Spoken words are invisible (like the air, oxygen and "spirit") and so you can have a confusion of *words* and *spirit*. The Bible says: "In the beginning was the Word, and the Word was with God, and the Word was God. The same was in the beginning with God. All things were made by him." (John 1:1-3). We now know that spoken words are just waves of air molecules that are compressed by the vibrations of the vocal cords.

The early humans saw that when someone was burned that their "soul" (all the water vapor, gasses, etc) rose into the air. Therefore, heaven was "up." Nowadays, "Heaven" has come to mean someplace besides up, perhaps existing somewhere in another unseen dimension. That is because natural philosophers and scientists have slowly shown over the last few centuries that what's "up" is not heaven, but the airless Moon, the hot stars, and barren and generally inhospitable planets.

The "*holy* spirit" is then the "*whole* oxygen" that surrounds us and is about 65% of living things and 47% of the Earth's crust. The "Father, Son, and Holy Spirit" of Catholicism were probably originally: 1) the volcano (such as Osiris), 2) the volcano resurrected (Horus the son), and 3) oxygen.

I was listening to a woman insisting, "God is here and now," and that she somehow senses Its presence. I believe that she was referring to what we call oxygen, but is still stuck in the primitive paradigm that has pervaded culture for millennia.

Some people, such as Carl Jung, said they felt there is a God because they sometimes got an "oceanic feeling." Although this could be interpreted as a regression to the aquatic womb, it could also be interpreted as simply being aware of the "ocean" of air in which we live. This atmosphere is readily visible from space. Feeling the air blowing on your skin, and the subtle changes in air pressure (some people can detect air pressure in their joints) would be the same as sensing the ocean of air around you. So this "oceanic feeling" is not really sensing the presence of God unless you define God as oxygen, which the early humans did.

The ancients aspired to be like this oxygen, apparently eternal and unconditionally loving.

We can now understand another conclusion that many mystics have come to — that you cannot live on the spirit (oxygen) alone. You need something to combine with the oxygen. We know now that the human body requires oxygen to burn the fuel that it gets from carbon-hydrogen-oxygen compounds (carbohydrates), which were built by plants, using the energy of the Home Star. The mystics who came to this conclusion were reporting their primitive scientific explorations to others. They were proto-scientists.

(Scientists do not like to be reminded that they owe a debt to mythology and religion. They are like teenagers who are embarrassed to be seen with their parents. They want their parents to drop them off a block before the gym where the school dance is being held. Scientists want to dance with the public and not acknowledge the debt they owe to the past—to the shamans, medicine men, alchemists, spiritualists, and priests.)

The Three Planes

Most early humans divided the world onto three planes: 1) below the earth, 2) the earth, 3) the heavens.

Up was good to the ancients because those who were taller were generally more powerful and survived better. *Up* was good because the life-giving Sun-God and Spirit-God were up. *Up* was good because life-giving water fell from above. *Up* was good because the life-giving fresh water rivers came from higher up. *Up* was good because the beautiful stars and planets were up. *Down* was bad because of the burning fire there. *Down* was bad because the lava pits gave off poisonous sulfur gasses. (When I visited the volcano on Hawaii, I camped in the Hawaiian Volcano National Park one night. By about 2 am, I was coughing and nauseous. I had to pack up my things and leave the park, because of the sulfurous fumes.) *Down* was bad because when you succumbed, you fell down.

In some religions, *down* became associated with evil and the "devil." If you were bad while you lived on earth, you went *down* to hell, and if you were good, you went *up* to heaven.

Of course, now we know that there is no "up" or "down." These words are like the word "sunset." They represent false models of reality. There is only "in" and "out." *In*, towards the center of the spherical Earth, and *out* away from the center of the spherical Earth. (As Bucky Fuller explained, airline pilots talk correctly about going *in* for a landing, not down.)

There is no "devil" at the center of the Earth. Everyone's atoms upon death are separated and recycled, sometimes slowly, sometimes rapidly, into the Earth's biosphere. Some atoms may go *in* and some may go *out* depending on the particular nature of your ending.

Before Galileo and Newton, and in the minds of the early humans, the earth was imperfect and the heavens were perfect. The perfect stars didn't *change*. They were always present, always shining, and always the same. (Except for the few "wandering stars," or planets that did not follow the pattern of the others.) The earth *changed*. Rocks crumbled away. People died. All (rigid) material things eventually died, weathered, corroded, or decomposed into a (non-rigid) nothingness in the air. Only the stars shone on, forever. (Galileo's daughter, a nun, after hearing of his imprisonment said, "And since you, by virtue of your vast experience, can lay claim to full cognizance of the fallacy and instability of everything in this miserable world...")

So the air "above" ground contained God or the spirits of their ancestors. "Above" that were the lights of the heavens. The spirits went "up" to this perfect heaven when they died, or (sometimes) down to hell.

The earth was the plane of passion, of desire, and of lust. This is where men spent their lives building empires and cities only to die

113

and have the cities crumble. The famous poem by Shelley, "Ozymandias of Egypt," comes to mind with the poignant line,

My name is Ozymandias, king of kings:
Look on my works, ye mighty, and despair!

Galileo then showed us that the heavens were not so perfect. There were mountains on the Moon, spots blemishing the face of the Sun, several moons orbiting around Jupiter. The "heavens" seemed more like our ordinary, imperfect world!

Newton's law of gravity, one simple law, then described quite well the motion of bodies in the heavens *and* on Earth. It described the motion of the Moon as well as the falling motion of an apple. The heavens and the Earth, for the first time, seemed almost the same.

The "heavens" (where we are embedded) are places of cataclysmic change. We know now that the stars are not eternal. They have a life-cycle. Also, comets and asteroids are swinging through the solar system sometimes crashing into planets, including ours. As you probably know, a large asteroid impact may have caused the extinction of the dinosaurs. Long before that, a large planet may have crashed into Earth, resulting in the formation of the Pacific Ocean and from the debris, our Moon.

Because these heavenly changes happen on such a slow scale compared to our human lives, the heavens can seem calm and beautiful (and perfect) from Earth. Thus, many early humans decided that earthly passions were bad. The "desires of the flesh" were desires that led to death and suffering. (Buddha's First Noble Truth: all life is suffering.) According to these people, we are all sinners, as we all have desires and passions for flesh, food, and other material things that eventually decompose or die. However, when early humans compared this ever-changing earthly "plane" of suffering to the (apparently) eternal and unchanging oxygen and stars, they decided that it was better to emulate yielding, nurturing and eternal spirit and the perfect fires in the heavens.

Fasting

Fasting is an important part of many religions. It is a time to renounce these material passions and earthly desires and to just breathe in the Oxygen "God" (of the higher plane).

It turns out that fasting may help to cleanse the system of unmetabolized waste products that accumulate.[190] It is a natural instinct of animals to fast when they are sick. We have lost that instinct; perhaps because of the huge barrage of advertising that tells us we need all manner of drugs and processed and cooked foods.

We now know that there is no miracle involved in fasting. In the old paradigm, it is the "holy spirit" healing us, as we renounce "earthly" pleasures of the senses. In the modern scientific paradigm, it is oxygen metabolizing (oxidizing) wastes products that have accumulated in the joints and elsewhere.[191]

We now know that our genes impel us to eat, drink and have sex. It is natural to do these things. We now know that the heavens are not "up" there anywhere, but that they *include* this Earth, which is a crusted-over heap of hot matter, circling round a minor star, in the boondocks of the galaxy. We are a *part* of the cosmos.

Homeostasis

It was discovered in the middle of the 20th Century that engineers could design systems that exhibited "goals." These were called *control systems*. A thermostat is an example. You set it to 70 degrees. When the temperature goes above 70, the air conditioning kicks in, and when the temperature goes below 70, the heater turns on. The result? It appears to have the "goal" of keeping the temperature at 70 degrees, no matter what.

Humans also have a control system for temperature regulation. We sweat when we get too hot, and we shiver and get "goose bumps" when we get too cold.

This demonstrates *homeostasis*. Homeostasis shows that *goal directed behavior does not require a mystical or supernatural power.* In other words, just because humans exhibit *goals* or *purposes* does not mean they are somehow different from inanimate objects.

This idea has important implications for human behavior and thought. Human behavior can be modeled using this idea of homeostasis. Who sets the "thermostat" for humans? Our genes, to a large degree. In other words, our genes have programmed us to have certain homeostatic "set points," for food, water, body temperature and sex, and this probably extends into the psychological domain.[192]

Humans have a larger range of motion than a machine temperature regulation system, which uses a thermostat. This doesn't mean that our goals are fundamentally different. A machine could be designed that had motion such as a robot vacuum cleaner whose homeostatic "set point" was a floor free of a certain amount of debris.

I think life could be called the result of a genetic recipe for a pattern of energy, that helps to bring homeostasis to larger systems.

Energism

The word *materialism* has some negative aspects. Materialism as a philosophy extends back to the ancient Greeks. In the 18th and 19th centuries, it was given new life by French and German writers. It is generally associated in our minds, due to ancient misconceptions, with rigid objects. The air was considered nonmaterial or "spiritual." It took a long time for humanity to realize that air was *matter,* which could be compressed, combined with other substances, etc.

The primitive idea of "disembodied entities" took hold in our minds. With each breath, we instinctively know that we are made of more than rigid bones and flesh. So, the common person scoffs at the philosophy of materialism.[193]

In addition, *the brain has no senses of itself. One can operate on the brain without using anesthesia on it.* Thus, the brain makes models of the world around it, but it cannot make a model of itself. It feels no pain. Even though the body is sick, the brain is feeling nothing. For this reason, one also tends to think that one is separate from the body.[194]

The word "naturalism" doesn't have the negative connotations of materialism. However, it was in 1905 that Einstein showed the equivalence of matter and energy. Matter is a sort of frozen or slowed down energy. The word "energy" generally has a positive connotation. We all like energy. *Energism* as a philosophy might establish a firm foothold in the human mind. Perhaps we should replace the word *naturalism* or *materialism* by the word *energism.*

Summary

What was named the "soul" or "spirit" was an attempt by early humans to understand what we now call oxygen and it's biological cycle.

Region	Oxygen Name
Egypt	Ba
China	Qi; Tao
Greece	Psyche
Japan	Reiki
India	Prana
Hebrew	Ruach

Primitive cultures over the course of many millennia were able to observe some obvious and important things about sustaining human life: 1) humans die when their blood flows out, 2) humans die when they can't breath, 3) blood evaporates into the thin air, and 4) burned human bodies reduce to a handful of ashes. They attempted to describe these events the best they could.

The ancients, to an extent, were trying to describe what science calls "water vapor," "oxygen," "hydrogen," and other gasses contained in the body and the air. The ancients deduced (incorrectly) that these invisible phenomena were somehow organized into personal units. They probably even deduced (correctly) that this *something-in-the-air* that is important to life gets into *the red-life-liquid* through breathing.

Most of the time when you see the word "spirit," you can substitute "blood," or "oxygen," (which is in the blood) and the sentence will make some sense. Many times when you see the word "soul," you can substitute "oxygen," "oxygen supply," "respiration," "breathing," "atmospheric oxygen," or "biosphere oxygen," and again the sentence makes some sense. Of course, now we know that the oxygen in the body is controlled by DNA and environmentally initiated actions.

Of course, as I said, the early humans were wrong when they thought that the individual had a *personal* "spirit" and "soul" that uniquely belonged to him or her. However, we should not judge those early humans too harshly. After all, every model (including atomic theory) is an approximation (however close) of the events occurring in the surrounding environment.[195]

Here is a chart summarizing the findings including the ancient Egyptian:

Religious	Ancient Egyptian	Descriptive	Scientific
Spirit	Ka	Invisible-formless-and-personal-life-giver-in the-air-(that-enters-the-red-life-liquid)	Oxygen, Blood, & interrelations
Soul	Ba	Invisible-formless-and-personal-life-giver-in-the-air-(that-enters-the-chest)	Oxygen & its interrelations

Several times, we have mentioned an important point. Water vapor and oxygen both have invisible and formless aspects to them. Note that light is also invisible. You only see it when it bounces off

117

something, such as particles of dust in the air, a rock or something else. Unfortunately, this gives a "mystical" or "supernatural" quality to knowledge (*meta*-physics or *beyond*-the-physical) that we have been saddled with ever since. In my opinion, this spills over into modern physics with its "higher dimensions." In fact, there is nothing *super*-natural or *meta*-physical. If something occurs, it is part of nature and responds to natural laws. Paul Kurtz coined the neat phrase "transcendental temptation," to describe the temptation to jump to a supernatural or transcendent explanation of inexplicable events. I think the invisible nature of what we call oxygen helps explain the origin and prevalence of this temptation.

Cultures sometimes used only one of the two terms (soul or spirit) and sometimes used two (like the Egyptians). The fact that we confuse these two terms is due to a) blood is supplied with oxygen by the breath and b) both water vapor and oxygen are invisible.

The Nile River Valley humans, believing they knew the two fundamental principles of human life, the *invisible-formless-and-personal-life-giver-in-the-air-(that-enters-the-red-life-liquid)*, or Ka, and the *invisible-formless-and-personal-life-giver-in-the-air-(that-enters-the-chest)*, or Ba, and thinking that they could prevent death, rottenness and decay through mummification, believed they might achieve immortality.

The ancient Nile River Valley people put the mummified Pharaoh and his vital organs inside a pyramid. Air shafts in the pyramid made sure that the *invisible-life-in-the-air*, or Ba, could re-animate him when the time came. Of course, the time never came.

So, still buried beneath the swirling sands of the Nile desert, or neatly displayed in glass-enclosed museum cases throughout the world, mummified Pharaohs yet wait for their Ka and Ba to return to reanimate them. However, their Ba will not return, because it is mostly what we now call oxygen.

Today, somewhat like the ancients, some scientists feel that by understanding human DNA and genes, they might also achieve immortality for humanity. Thanks to previous work by Darwin, Mendel, Crick, Watson and now others such as Aubrey de Grey, we have begun to understand cell maintenance technology.

Also, perhaps one day we will take some DNA of a Pharaoh and be able to create a clone. In a roundabout way, the Pharaoh might get his wish. However, we can duplicate the exact genes, but never the exact environment. So, it will not be the same Pharaoh. It will just be a genetic copy that is dropped into an utterly different environment.

There is no Santa Claus, no tooth fairy, no Easter Bunny. The "mothership" is really just a studio prop or computer animation, the sun doesn't "set," and your individual "spirit" or "soul," although in a sense they leave your body at death, cannot somehow be returned to "you," a unique personality, at another time through "reincarnation." An individual's personality is forged from their very particular genes, and their very particular environment, and for any two individuals these are never the same, ever.[196] Take the cold bath.

Who knows how long ago the *invisible-life-giver-in-the-air* was first observed, isolated, codified, and thus made part of human knowledge? Perhaps when language first developed. A current estimate for this is 350,000 years ago, as that was when the position of the larynx may have moved lower, allowing for greater vocalization.

Yet, it is only in the last 100 years of this immense span that we have developed the atomic model. Physicist Richard Feynman summarized the importance of this discovery:

If, in some cataclysm, all of scientific knowledge were to be destroyed, and only one sentence passed on to the next generation of creatures, what statement would contain the most information in the fewest words? I believe it is the *atomic hypothesis ... all things are made of atoms...*[197]

Oxygen makes up, surrounds, and gives life to humanity. It allows the biosphere (some call it Gaia) to continue. *Humanity, by saying, "soul" and "spirit," is using ideas that allow it to symbolize, in a way that does not require knowledge of atomic theory, the extremely vital substance "oxygen."*

There exists what I call a "spiral of knowledge." What in the past was "soul," "spirit," and *"the-invisible-god-in-the-air,"* becomes in our current theory (further out along the spiral) "oxygen."

Note that our current atomic model (around the turn of the millennia, 2000 AD) may someday be replaced by a more comprehensive model, as far removed from atomic theory as atomic theory is removed from the "soul and spirit theory."

Alchemy	Chemistry	Future Chemistry
fire-earth-air-water	about 118 elements in the atomic array	?

In other words, atomic theory may look to future scientists

much as the "soul" and "spirit" look to many people today — as primitive superstitious or religious beliefs. (Perhaps "atomic theory" will be worshiped [198] by future "religions" or organizational structures.) Thus, it is doubtful that Tylor's Dream Theory is correct. How many of us think that because we dream something that it might exist somewhere? Tylor had too low a view of the deductive and observational powers of ancient humans. As I said, they (humans of 50,000 years ago) had a similar brain capacity as we do. [199]

I think it is hard for the scientific model (as we enter the third millennium) to displace the ideas of "soul" and/or "spirit" and "God" because of two factors:

1) The tremendous cultural momentum of these early concepts, having perhaps 50,000 to 1,000,000 years of history behind them as compared with only 100 or so years for the atomic theory. For many generations, "soul" and "spirit" have been taught to children (using the "belief module" of the brain), made part of sacred texts, and have even become ingrained into our language to the point where they are now an *unexamined background assumption.* When looked at from this standpoint, science has made enormous progress in just a few years.

2) The simplicity (and relative inaccuracy) of the "soul/spirit" model as compared with the "atomic theory" model. This simplicity allows people to avoid having to learn the more complex (and more accurate) array of chemical elements and how they interact.

Does the idea of the soul/spirit have any adaptive significance? In other words—of what survival value to the genes are these ideas and the resulting behaviors? Well, one survival value of having an idea of the "soul" or of the "Great Spirit" would be the same survival value held by any science or knowledge. The knowledge helps the individual and culture to understand and deal with the surrounding world. In this case, it may have provided a clue how to dispose of dead, decaying bodies. Also, when combined with knowledge of volcanoes and sulfur, the knowledge of the "soul" led to alchemy, and then to chemistry and then to the atomic theory and oxygen.

So at death, in the scientific model, the "spirit" does not leave the body. The blood flow stops, the body ceases to take in water, and the water in the blood leaves the body, or evaporates.

At death, in the scientific model, the "soul" of the person does not leave the body. We now might say the body ceases functioning, or that the cells age and eventually die, and respiration stops. His or her atoms, which are mostly oxygen, are eventually

120

recycled as part the vast web of life we call the biosphere. The personal "soul" and "spirit" reveal themselves to be part of a vast, shared, soup of atoms.

9 ☼

Connecting the Dots

A religion, old or new, that stressed the magnificence of the Universe as revealed by modern science might be able to draw forth reserves of reverence and awe hardly tapped by the conventional faiths.

Carl Sagan

Human Evolution

Life probably formed in the oceans near the dynamic volcanic vents that release hot chemicals into the ocean. Early life took energy from this. Life eventually evolved to take energy from the Sun.

Certain forms of life were selected to survive over others because they had a reproductive advantage of some sort. We say they were "better fit" to the surrounding environment or better "adapted." Meanwhile, other forms of life were eliminated.

Of course, life also selected and changed the environment, so a coevolutionary process has been going on. The Earth has maintained the same temperature despite the Home Star increasing its output by 25%. James Lovelock documents this in *The Ages of Gaia*. It is homeostasis at work on a planetary level.

Lyn Margulis proposes that the reason we have complex life is simply to equalize the differential energy gradient.[200] This works something like a tornado. A tornado exists to dispel differential pressures. A high pressure in one area and a low pressure in another area are equalized by the means of a tornado. Likewise, life helps to

123

equalize the energy differences between the solar output of the Sun and the coldness of space. This could even function on a galactic or higher level: a galactic homeostasis or a universal homeostasis.

Eventually, in the area we now know as Southeast Asia, primates called lemurs evolved. These lemurs differentiated into other primates, which were the common ancestors of apes and humans. These ape-like primates lived in the forest and jungles of Asia and Africa.

During the ice ages, over the last two million years, the ocean level sank leaving large areas of land exposed, including plains and land bridges that connected many of the tens of thousands of islands in Southeast Asia to the mainland. Perhaps the ape-like primates wandered into the lush tropical forests, which now existed on these connected areas. When the ice age came, the ocean level sank, the land bridges disappeared, and these primates were cut off from the main continent and from larger islands.

Since most of these islands were volcanic (lying on the Ring of Fire or the Australian-Eurasian plate boundary) eventually they erupted, spewing tons of ash, lava, hot mudflows, and/or poisonous gasses onto the islands. Perhaps all the food on the island disappeared or perhaps the lava overwhelmed the island. For whatever reason, the ape-like primates were forced into the sea and eventually, over perhaps a few million years, those that had 1) the most erect posture for keeping the head above water, 2) little hair for ease of swimming, 3) a subcutaneous layer of fat (found in no apes but found in other aquatic mammals such as sea lions, whales, etc.), 4) a hand similar to the American raccoon, 5) speech complexity comparable to that of the dolphins and whales, etc. were selected as being more fit to this new environment. In short, we have an "aquatic ape," a theory put forth first by Sir Alister Hardy and later elaborated upon by Elaine Morgan in *The Aquatic Ape* and other books. This evolutionary process could have occurred in South East Asia, or in Africa on Danakil Island off the coast of Ethiopia.[201]

Seafaring Humans

Of course, during this time, the evolving humans eventually learned how to build rafts and to navigate from island to island or from island to mainland. To these people the world was *obviously* curved and was *obviously* a sphere, as they could see every time they left one island and went to the next, how the island would slowly "sink" below the horizon. To landlocked people, the mountains, hills, and trees block the view of this sight. Also, the use of many flat maps tends to make us think and feel of the world as flat.[202]

About 50,000 years ago these people had a similar brain capacity as we do today. It would have been easy for them to develop a technology of stellar navigation, ocean current navigation, and even trigonometry. Some of this lore exists today as Polynesian chants and navigation charts, an elaborate and intricate system of knowledge and navigation. I confirmed this when I was in Hawaii and visited ancient archeological sites and talked with one of the few remaining Kahunas.[203]

Unfortunately, humans returning from Africa and Asia to Europe would try to describe monkeys, and we got "elves" instead. They tried to describe rhinos and we got "unicorns" instead. They tried to describe lava bombs, and we got "angels" instead.

Volcanoes

The "Big Island" of Hawaii contains 53 of the 54 possible ecosystems. It was amazing to drive around and see surroundings identical to those I had experienced far away, where I grew up in Illinois. Here, I first began to see the importance of volcanic origins for all life. I visited the live, flowing volcano of Kilauea and stood a few feet from the hot lava as it flowed into the ocean and created rock and new land before my eyes. I had never had such a profound an experience as this.

The early humans had thousands and thousands of years of using their high capacity brains in which to observe and travel among the volcanic islands. The *tens of thousands* of years (or more) of observation enabled these people to witness volcanoes breaking through the surface of the ocean, or large lakes (such as Lake Turkana in East Africa) and forming new land. This was a key observation. It probably resulted in the story of a creation in seven days. They probably also witnessed the gradual development of plants and animals on these newly forming islands. They saw the entire world apparently blossom forth from undifferentiated rock and ash.

Tens of thousands of years observations of these islands allowed these people to develop a proto-science that described for them the creation and destruction of life. To these people God was the Volcano God. This God lived *inside* the Earth. The Gods of the Sun, Moon, and stars existed as related Gods who took their nourishment from the Volcano God when they went "beneath" the horizon each night.

Also, the early humans saw the huge outgassing of volcanoes and hypothesized (correctly) that the atmosphere came also from the Volcano God. They probably hypothesized (incorrectly) that the stars and other heavenly bodies resulted from volcanic ash and gas being spewed upward (along with the rising of their ancestors' "spirits").

Seeing a volcano rise up out of the sea, life blossom forth, the volcano disappear again into the sea, and then a new volcano rise up where the old one was, enabled them to conjecture that this cycle was the cycle of all things. This philosophy still exists in the Hindu pantheon. The cycle of creation, life, destruction, and then creation again, enabled some of them to conjecture that all things, people included, are born from ocean depths by the lava that spews forth, then eventually returned to the ocean depths perhaps to be reborn again. Thus, one idea of reincarnation was born.

Another idea of reincarnation would be a recycling of human spirits. The ancients found that many things could be burned and turned into air: logs, people, and animals, etc. Oxygen is even the most abundant element in the Earth's crust making up 47%.

These early humans probably postulated that lower forms of life gave way to higher (more complex) form of life. So again we have the idea of reincarnation, which is a primitive (though inaccurate) version of evolution.

Records of these early human travels are not so easily discovered since their bamboo and wooden rafts (and later boats) do not preserve like stone. Stone preserves so easily that archeologists, somewhat in error, call this early period the "stone age." Also, since land preserves things better than salt water, archeologists have primarily studied land peoples and all our history is somewhat skewed because of this. We also have the popular misnomer "cave man." This probably doesn't capture the seafaring and shipbuilding capabilities of these people. In reality, we probably had a hunter, gatherer, *and* seafarer.

Because these people frequently saw molten lava turned to stone when it contacted the ocean, their high capacity brains were able to eventually recognize that the process could be reversed and that stone (and eventually metals) could be turned to liquid. They developed a technology around this and were able to pour large stone structures (now called geopolymerization), which eventually resulted in the Great Pyramids in Egypt.[204]

Pyramids were constructed in the old world and the new world, in an attempt to represent the vital knowledge of the most creative and most destructive power the ancients had seen--

volcanoes.

Pyramids in Egypt were designed to send the Pharaoh into the company of Gods. Since the original early humans believed that God lived deep inside the volcano, people of many lands built pyramids to represent the volcano. This was an attempt to control nature, and more specifically, death. They elected one of their own people (the Pharaoh for example) to represent the Volcano God and when he died the Pharaoh was put into the center of the volcano where the God would normally live.

At first, early humans passed along their creation science orally. Later, they developed a pictorial-type language (early hieroglyphs) and documented their science on stone or clay tablets. *Genesis* of the Christian and Jewish sacred texts and the *Koran* derive from these early observations and stories.

The science of alchemy developed, which later became chemistry. The word alchemy derives from the ram-headed god of Egypt, Khnum, and perhaps earlier from kemit, which means black soil, which probably came from the black volcanic soil. The "philosopher's stone" was said to be a "stone that was not a stone." In other words, like liquid lava. It was said to exist among the most "foul things." In other words, among the sulfurous gases escaping from volcanic vents. It was capable of being turned into gold. This is true, as today the rich copper-gold ore deposits in eastern Indonesia (which come from magma) are melted and then the gold and copper is skimmed off the top.

Seeing all the volcanic islands and the magma spewing forth, winding down the side of the volcano, the early humans were reminded of the curving undulations of a snake. Thus the persistent legend of a serpent or dragon was born. Also, the fire that the volcanoes occasionally belched forth became the fire-breath of the sea serpent.

The early humans developed an elaborate science (or theology) around the Volcano God. The fiery "lava bombs" of the volcano were seen as messengers of the Volcano God. These are the basis of angels. The supreme deity of Bali (the island next to Java and as early as 30,000 years ago a part of Java) is pictured as a man with flames coming out of him, inside a burning ember, flying through the sky, to the earth. (See photo at front of book.)

The early humans also observed, with great grief, the volcano take human lives. The people incorrectly conjectured that the Volcano God needed human lives and they eventually decided to give the God what it wanted in the hopes that it would be appeased. This eventually took the form of highly elaborate ritualistic human sacrifice in which humans were thrown into craters and lakes of lava. This sacrifice was still being practiced on some parts of Sumatra when Europeans arrived there in the 1600s.

A volcano probably was rumbling for several months before its final explosion. (This is what happened at Krakatau during its 1883 explosion.) To certain local people the Volcano God was communicating. Possibly one individual correctly interpreted the rumblings as the fact that the volcano was about to violently explode. He therefore built not a ship, but an ark, a ship with *cover*, (the Hebrew word for ark means a "floating palace") as he knew that the ash from the explosion would be dangerous and probably lethal. To this day, in Southern Java, one village every year sets afloat small ceremonial houseboats or palaces into the Indian Ocean as part of a religious festival.[205] Some later translators possibly misinterpreted the ashes that rained down as *liquid* rain. Also, "...ash particles in the atmosphere...act as condensation nuclei ('cloud seeding') for water vapor"[206] so rain may have fallen also.

Noah's story, or a flood legend, is found in the sacred texts of the Egyptians, Babylonians, Hebrews, Christians, Moslems, and many other cultures around the world. It was considered sacred because it was an attempt to keep this knowledge alive, to prevent a similar devastation from occurring in the future. However, along with this knowledge came the teachings that this type of volcanic activity is repeated or cyclical. Therefore we also have the legend of the so-called Judgment Day, which in reality is nothing more than a violent volcanic eruption or some other geological act such as a tsunami, repeating itself and again wiping out the entire surrounding environment.

The "myths" of the Greeks, Romans, Egyptians, Mayans, etc., were mostly derived from attempts to describe volcanoes and oxygen and to provide and Grand Unified Theory of Light. The Light from Lightning was probably thought of as a *connection* between the Light in the Heavens (Sun, Moon, Jupiter, Stars, etc.) and the Light of Earth (magma-lava, fire).

These myths provide a record of the accumulated observation and knowledge of at least tens of thousands of years. They were also an attempt to explain the creation of land and life on the land. They are a kind of anthropological and geological history.

Like the Polynesian people, other early humans chanted their knowledge. Much later it was recorded on stones. Homer's poems were originally chanted before being written down.

There probably was considerable travel between the Occident, a word derived from "the fall" (of the sun) (i.e., Europe and Africa), and the Orient, a word derived from "the rise" (of the sun) (i.e., Asia and Indonesia). All this was the "Old World," and one could move from one part of it to another in a boat without getting too far from land.

The Old World as Seen by the Early Humans

Occident	Orient
Europe and Africa	Indochina, Indonesia, Japan, China
Land of the setting sun	Land of the rising sun

In India, the revolutionary Gautama Siddhartha, better known as the Buddha, perhaps having seen no island volcanoes or angels, broke somewhat with the Hindu reincarnation idea. He taught that only "strands of desire" are left of a person after death. His knowledge was based more on the search to understand oxygen than on the search to understand volcanoes. He also left us with the idea, derived from his observations of the "material plane" that all things are *impermanent*.

In Mexico and Central America, the earth was geologically similar to Indonesia and the Sunda Plain.[207] This area is on the "Ring of Fire," a large circular crack in the crust that extends around the periphery of the Pacific. Here in Mesoamerica the Volcano God was everywhere, and bloody sacrifice was practiced to appease the God. The Aztecs once sacrificed 60,000 people in one day.

One of the most interesting moments in history occurring when the Spanish Christians came to the new world and met the Aztecs.[208] The Spanish had a religion that had become almost completely removed from its volcanic beginnings. This religion met a religion that was still, incorrectly and destructively, connected to volcanoes.

About this time, Galileo and others began the modern scientific movement. Newton, Dalton, and Darwin made great advances in understanding motion, the atom, and life. Experimentation had begun to replace authoritarianism. The Scientific Renaissance in Europe had begun.

Connecting the Dots

It is relatively warm evening in Southern California. The Earth has spun so that it faces away from our Home Star. Invited by a well-meaning friend, I sit in a large stone cathedral near the sea, on the night before what is called "Easter." To me it is Easter, the time Earth faces the Home Star in such a way as to cause it to appear directly east, and cause a renewal of life in the populated Northern Hemisphere.

In the front of the church stands the altar, that ancient place of ritual sacrificial burning, and from behind it the modern holy man speaks. The lights are out now. The air circulates freely through the open doors of the cathedral and up and down the aisles. I hold a candle, its flame flickering in the air. Throughout the enclosure a thousand other flames dance to the rhythm of the air, held by faces only dimly seen.

I look up at the high ceiling where there are large, ornate windows of stained glass. Many years ago, my fellow hominids gathered up the earth, various metals and stone, and fashioned them into this large "spiritual" cave, perhaps representing a hollowed-out pyramid.

I recall the Great Pyramids, the largest human-made structures of the ancient world, built to represent volcanoes and the God of the underworld and to show us their power to create as well as destroy, and how we humans could forget and allow hundreds of thousands to die in a tsunami.

Now, in the front of the cave, some hominids are being dipped into a large bath of water. Surrounding me is the ancient foursome: Air. Earth. Fire. Water. I stare in wonder, feeling somewhat like an anthropologist from the future observing a primitive ritual.

Appendix A: Timeline

This timeline is not an attempt to be an exhaustive survey. It merely serves to give some historical perspective to some of the things that have been discussed in this book. Some dates and items are subject to change based on future information.

3.8 billion bp:(before present) First life on Earth. Life may have developed in the deep hot biosphere or volcanic vents on the ocean floor.

2.4 billion bp: The Great Oxidation Event. Earth's atmosphere changes radically, and becomes saturated with oxygen (O_2) for the first time, allowing the rise of complex cells, multicellular life, and air-breathing animal life.

65,000,000 bp: Comet or asteroid impact (and resulting volcanic activity) may have led to the extinction of the dinosaurs and allowed for mammals to flourish in the empty ecological niches.

6,000,000 bp: Split of chimpanzee ancestors and our ancestors in the Old World.

2,000,000 bp: The ice ages begin on planet Earth perhaps driven by interstellar dust or perhaps certain oscillations in the Earth-Sun system. Since this time the Earth has been more often in an ice age than not. Some scientists feel that these ice ages may have triggered the beginning of the *Homo* genus, or humanity.

1,800,000 bp: *Homo erectus* migrates rapidly to Asia and Indonesia.

1,000,000 bp: Regular oscillations in the ice ages are evident. During the ice ages great areas, such as the Sunda Plain, are laid bare that are now under the ocean. The volcano Krakatau may have had mega eruptions periodically— about once every 100,000 years.

800,000-900,000 bp: the first ocean voyages, according to archeologist Robert Bednarick.

800,000 bp: Some evidence that *Homo erectus* existed on Flores Island, Indonesia. They may have used sea craft to get to the island. **600,000 bp:** Yellowstone mega-volcano explodes. No humans in the New World to see it. 800,000 – 600,000-year cycle. Last explosion before this was 1.2 million years ago. We are about due for another one.

1,000,000-500,000 bp: Fire is domesticated by *Homo sapiens*.

500,000 bp: Domestication of dogs.

400,000 bp: Weighted wooden spears found in Shonongen, China.

350,000 bp: Stone hand ax may have been buried with dead in a Spanish cavern. Suggests thoughts of an afterlife.

300,000-200,000 bp: The beginnings of modern speech may have occurred somewhere in this time span due to the change of the location of the larynx.

100,000 bp: The most recent ice age begins. The *Homo* species further differentiated into what we call *Homo sapiens*. Symbolic burial site, decorated with red dye, in Qafzeh Cave.

75,000 bp: A volcano in northern Sumatra explodes violently, one of the largest explosions ever of a volcano, leaving behind today's huge Lake Toba. A 5 degree Celsius temperature drop worldwide. This event probably killed a majority of the human population and thus reduced genetic diversity by forming a DNA bottleneck.

63,000 bp: Ram figurine made (and found in Israel).

60,000 bp: The peopling of Australia.

30,000 bp: Notches on bones suggest the beginning of a primitive mathematical writing.

20,000-13,000 bp: The first peopling of the North and South America.

18,000 bp: The most recent ice age reaches its glacial maximum. Ocean levels would have been the lowest in many years, exposing vast areas of all the oceans including the area between Indonesia, South East Asia and the Philippines.

12,000 bp: The time when Plato says that "Atlantis" was destroyed. The beginning of the rapid end of the ice age.

10,000 bp: Beginnings of agriculture, and thus specialization, stratification and religion. Egalitarian spiritual tribes are replaced by hierarchical, religious nation-states. Planting of bananas in New Guinea. Bronze smelting.

12,000-5000 bp: The volcano Krakatau may have erupted violently around this time, leading to an oral legend of flood and fiery destruction throughout the Old World.

5000 BCE: (Before the Common Era) The beginnings of written language in China and Nile River Valley. This allowed a written record of civilization.

2700 BCE: Rise of the big pyramids in Egypt.

1628 BCE: The violent eruption of the island Thera (Santorini volcano) in the Mediterranean. May have been responsible for the fall of civilization on Crete. May have been responsible for certain events mentioned in *Exodus* such as the parting of the Red Sea, etc. Evidence exists that it explodes periodically.

600 BCE: The arrival of Buddhism and Greek rationalism. Buddha creates a prescientific psychology. Socrates also promotes rational thought, rather than primitive volcano worship.

350 BCE Aristotle writes *De Anima* (*On the Soul*). An attempt at a logical analysis of the soul.

3 CE: (Common Era): "Jesus" is allegedly born, but may have been based on an Osiris-type resurrection, which was probably based on observations of the growth of a new volcano in the place of the exploded one.

535 CE: A possible eruption of Krakatau at this time may have had a major influence on modern history. According to David Keys, due to the cooler climate, rats proliferated and the plague spread out of Africa. This may have precipitated the collapse of the Roman Empire.

600 CE: Mohammed starts Islam, which has an invisible God.

1000 CE: Sunda Strait, site of Krakatau, is navigable again.

1006 CE: An eruption of Merapi on Java probably ended the Hindu-Javanese kingdom of Mataram in central Java.

1268 CE: Thomas Aquinas begins writing *On the Soul*, commenting on the work of Aristotle. He maintains that the soul is the most substantial part of the body and survives after death.

1452-1519 CE: Renaissance man Leonardo da Vinci lives.

1492 CE: Columbus contacts the people of the Americas.

1473-1543 Copernicus suggests a Sun-centered planetary system.

1517-1546 CE: Martin Luther says salvation is a personal matter, between you and God alone.

1592 CE: Body dissection reveals that man and women have the same number of ribs, contrary to the Bible.

1600 CE: Europeans (Cortez) contact the Aztecs.

1564-1642 CE: Galileo champions Copernican Sun-centered system. Uses telescope to examine the heavens, develops preliminary laws of motion.

1654 CE: Biblical scholar James Usher states that the Earth was created in 4004 BCE.

1664 CE: Thomas Willis publishes *Cerebri anatomi,* a detailed anatomy of the human brain. He was the first to use the term "reflex action."

1642–1727 CE: Newton develops "law of gravity," and "laws of motion." Motion in the heavens shown to be subject to the same laws as motion on earth.

1728 CE: First cataloging of a dinosaur bone by John Woodward; probably Megalosaurus. Evidence that some species may have died out. Many could not believe "God" had created things, pronounced them good, and then wiped them out.

1776 CE: Franklin, Washington, Jefferson, and others attempt to launch a nation based on enlightened, scientific principles, and which is more democratic than previous systems of government.

1783 CE: Lavoisier and others investigate and isolate the element oxygen. This clarified the relationship between oxygen and fire.

1785 CE: James Hutton's *Theory of the Earth* is published, which addresses the extended length of geological time.

1796 CE: Georges Cuvier recognizes, from the existence of fossils, that some species go extinct. Codeveloped the principle of biological succession.

1803 CE: Dalton develops the modern theory of atoms.

1859 CE: Charles Darwin's *The Origin of Species* is published. Later *The Descent of Man, The Expression of the Emotions in Man and Animals,* and other works. His books suggest that complexity can arise without any prior design or a supernatural guide.

1860s CE Louis Pasteur develops the germ theory of disease that helps replaces the demon theory of illness.

1863 CE: Sir Charles Lyell's (following James Hutton), *The Geological Evidence of the Antiquity of Man* is published, suggesting that human history is much older than 6,000 years as suggested by the Bible.

1857-1867 CE: Mendel does his experiments with peas and lays the foundation for the modern science of genetics.

1869 CE: Mendeleev creates a table of the elements, organizing them according to their periodic nature, which successfully predicts the discovery of new elements.

1883 CE: The volcano Krakatau explodes again, killing 36,000 in the resulting tidal wave.

1897 CE: J. J. Thompson announces discovery of the particles we now call electrons.

1905 CE: Einstein formulates the equality of matter and energy.

1911 CE: Rutherford develops the nuclear model of the atom.

1920s CE: The philosophy of "logical positivism" states that all knowledge comes from experience and logic, and thus metaphysical statements are completely meaningless.

1933 CE: Korzybski's *Science and Sanity* is published.

1930s CE: Engineers develop *control systems* for *homeostasis*, which seem to copy the "purposefulness" and "goals" of living things.

1939 CE: Freud's *Moses and Monotheism* is published, suggesting Moses was an Egyptian.

1945 CE: The explosion of the first atomic bomb: conversion of mass to energy.

1948 CE: Norbert Weiner applies control systems and homeostasis to human behavior in the book, *Cybernetics*.

1952 CE: The discovery of the structure of the DNA molecule by James Watson and Francis Crick. Provides a clear mechanism for copying hereditary material from one generation to the next.

1956 CE: Dartmouth College Artificial Intelligence Workshop.

1962 CE: Thomas Kuhn's *The Structure of Scientific Revolutions* is published, which describes scientific paradigms and scientific revolutions.

1964 CE: William Hamilton introduces the idea of "inclusive fitness" which explains altruism at a genetic level.

1981 CE: Bucky Fuller's *Critical Path* is published, which suggests prehistoric seafaring and circumnavigation.

1973 CE: William Powers' *Behavior: The Control of Perception* is published, which says that all living things are hierarchically organized feedback systems.

1984 CE: The Santa Fe Institute is founded to study "complex adaptive systems."

1986 CE: Eric Drexler publishes *Engines of Creation,* about molecular nanosystems.

1988 CE: James Lovelock's *The Ages of Gaia* is published, which suggests that homeostasis operates at the planetary level.

1988 CE: Davidovits' *The Pyramids: An Enigma Solved* is published, which suggests that stone blocks in the pyramids were poured, not hauled in a process known today as geopolymerization.

1990 Richard Dawkins' *The Selfish Gene* is published popularizing "inclusive fitness," the idea that people make sacrifices to help the identical genes that exist in others.

1992 CE: Mott C. Greene's *Natural Knowledge in Preclassical Antiquity* is published, which describes volcanic lightning and its role in Greek mythology.

1996 CE: Publication of *The Demon-Haunted World* by Carl Sagan. Examines pseudoscience and UFOs.

1997 CE: A computer, Deep Blue, defeats a world chess champion, Gary Kasparov.

1997 CE: Bill Lauritzen begins to publish the theory that religion and science evolved from 1) the study of the "heavens," 2) observations of geological catastrophes and phenomena, and 3) the search for what we call "oxygen." He predicts future catastrophes in the Indian Ocean near Indonesia.

2000 CE: First draft of the human genome.

2004 CE: In what might be called a "Judgment Day," or "end of the world" event, as predicted in early religious or mythological texts, geologically activity in the Indian Ocean near Indonesia produces a tsunami that kills over 225,000.

2004 CE: Publication of *On Intelligence,* by Jeff Hawkins, which gives a comprehensive framework of brain functioning.

2005 CE: Raymond Kurzweil publishes *The Singularity is Near,* which predicts super-intelligent machines and humans will merge and become immortal.

APPENDIX B: Chart of Ancient and Modern Knowledge

Event or Phenomenon	Ancient Knowledge	Modern Knowledge
creation of matter	Volcano God: volcanic islands and volcanic mountains	big bang, quantum fluctuations
creation of life, mankind	Volcano God: volcanic islands and volcanic mountains	deep hot biosphere, test tube life
Species creation	Volcano God (Divine Potter makes man out of clay)	natural selection
structure of matter	fire-earth-air-water, volcanic sulfur, fire-powder, alchemy	118 elements of the periodic table, chemistry
motion of the land	movement of the underground serpent	plate tectonics
Grand Unification Theory	fire-water-air-earth, or all things come from fire-light (Ra and Atum)	gravity, radiation, strong nuclear force, weak nuclear force
Breeding	artificial selection of plants (bananas, etc.) and animals (dogs, horses, etc.)	DNA mapping, genetic engineering, cloning, stem cells
the sky	motion of the Gods (planetary and star motion), eclipse prediction	gravity (curved spacetime), quasars, "black holes," relativity, extra-solar planetary discovery
construction	carpentry, cut stone, poured stone	geo-polymerization, carbon fibers, nanomaterials
Various invisible forces	sparks, falling-to-earth, lodestone	gravity waves, electromagnetism, superconductivity
breathing	connection with spirit, soul, God	intake of oxygen, exhale of carbon dioxide
motion of humans	moved by spirit, soul, or God	programmed by DNA and fueled by oxygen and the sun
human birth	flesh and bones with base material desires, but imbued with spirit or soul by God	atomic and molecular pattern that is programmed by genes for survival in past environments
human death	a return to natural and perfect state of spirit (in the air, in heaven, or in the underworld) or returned to flesh again (reincarnate)	biospheric, atomic, and molecular recycling
catastrophic destruction	angry Gods punishing humans in a "Judgment Day" event	statistically inevitable volcanoes, earthquakes, and comet/meteor impacts

APPENDIX C: Volcanic Glossary

Ash: Fine particles of pulverized rock blown from an explosion vent. Measuring less than 1/10 inch in diameter, ash may be either solid or molten when first erupted. By far the most common variety is glassy particles formed by gas bubbles bursting through liquid magma.

Ash Flow or Pyroclastic Flow: A turbulent mixture of gas and rock fragments, most of which are ash-sized particles, ejected violently from a crater or fissure. The mass of pyroclastics is normally of very high temperature and moves rapidly down the slopes or even along a level surface.

Caldera: The Spanish word for cauldron, a basin-shaped volcanic depression; by definition, at least a mile in diameter. Such large depressions are typically formed by the subsidence of volcanoes. Crater Lake occupies the best-known caldera in the Cascades.

Central Vent: A central vent is an opening at the Earth's surface of a volcanic conduit of cylindrical or pipe-like form.

Debris Flow: A mixture of water-saturated rock debris that flows downslope under the force of gravity (also called lahar or mudflow).

Ejecta: Material that is thrown out by a volcano, including pyroclastic material (tephra) and lava bombs.

Eruption: The process by which solid, liquid, and gaseous materials are ejected into the earth's atmosphere and onto the earth's surface by volcanic activity. Eruptions range from the quiet overflow of liquid rock to the tremendously violent expulsion of pyroclastics.

Flank Eruption: An eruption from the side of a volcano (in contrast to a summit eruption).

Fumarole: A vent or opening through which issue steam, hydrogen sulfide, or other gases. The craters of many dormant volcanoes contain active fumaroles.

Harmonic Tremor: A continuous release of seismic energy typically associated with the underground movement of magma. It contrasts distinctly with the sudden release and rapid decrease of seismic energy associated with the more common type of earthquake caused by slippage along a fault.

Horizontal Blast: An explosive eruption in which the resultant cloud of hot ash and other material moves laterally rather than upward.

Lapilli: Literally, "little stones." Round to angular rock fragments, measuring 1/10 inch to 2 1/2 inches in diameter, which may be ejected in either a solid or molten state.

Lava: Magma which has reached the surface through a volcanic eruption. The term is most commonly applied to streams of liquid rock that flow from a crater or fissure. It also refers to cooled and solidified rock.

Lava bomb: Fragment of molten or semi-molten rock, 2 1/2 inches to many feet in diameter, which is blown out during an eruption. Because of their plastic condition, bombs are often modified in shape during their flight or upon impact.

Lava Flow: An outpouring of lava onto the land surface from a vent or fissure. Also, a solidified tongue like or sheet like body formed by outpouring lava.

Lava Fountain: A rhythmic vertical fountain-like eruption of lava.

Lava Lake (Pond): A lake of molten lava, usually basaltic, contained in a vent, crater, or broad depression of a shield volcano.

Lithic: Of or pertaining to stone.

Lithosphere: The topmost layer of the Earth's structure, composed of the crust and part of the upper mantle. The lithosphere is broken up into plates that move across the Earth's surface.

Magma: Molten rock underneath the ground. Magma differs from lava in that lava is molten rock on the surface of the Earth, while magma is the same rock underneath the surface. Molten rock beneath the surface of the earth.

Magma Chamber: The subterranean cavity containing the gas-rich liquid magma which feeds a volcano.

Magmatic: Pertaining to magma.

Mudflow: A flowage of water-saturated earth material possessing a high degree of fluidity during movement. A less-saturated flowing mass is often called a debris flow. A mudflow originating on the flank of a volcano is properly called a lahar.

Outgassing: The release of gases, especially by volcanoes.

137

Volcanic Glossary

Pahoehoe: Hawaiian term for lava with a smooth, billowy, or ropy surface.

Parasitic cones: secondary or side vents.

Pele Hair: A natural spun glass formed by blowing-out during quiet fountaining of fluid lava, cascading lava falls, or turbulent flows, sometimes in association with pele tears. A single strand, with a diameter of less than half a millimeter, may be as long as two meters.

Phreatic Eruption (Explosion): An explosive volcanic eruption caused when water and heated volcanic rocks interact to produce a violent expulsion of steam and pulverized rocks. Magma is not involved.

Phreatomagmatic: An explosive volcanic eruption that results from the interaction of surface or subsurface water and magma.

Pillow lava: Interconnected, sack-like bodies of lava formed underwater.

Plate Tectonics: The theory that lithospheric plates move around the Earth's surface by riding on an elastic layer of mantle (the asthenosphere). Plate tectonics explains seafloor spreading, deep-sea trenches, and the locations of earthquakes, volcanoes, and mountains. The theory of plate tectonics was developed in the 1960s.

Plinian Eruption: An explosive eruption in which a steady, turbulent stream of fragmented magma and magmatic gases is released at a high velocity from a vent. Large volumes of tephra and tall eruption columns are characteristic.

Pyroclastic: Pertaining to fragmented (clastic) rock material formed by a volcanic explosion or ejection from a volcanic vent.

Pyroclastic Flow: Lateral flowage of a turbulent mixture of hot gases and unsorted pyroclastic material (volcanic fragments, crystals, ash, pumice, and glass shards) that can move at high speed (50 to 100 miles an hour). The term also can refer to the deposit so formed.

Ring of Fire: The regions of mountain-building earthquakes and volcanoes which surround the Pacific Ocean.

Seafloor Spreading: The growth of ocean floor out away from mid-ocean ridges as magma from within the Earth pushes through to the surface**Seafloor Spreading:** The mechanism by which new seafloor crust is created at oceanic ridges and slowly spreads away as plates are separating.

Seamount: Submarine volcano that does not at present rise above sea level.

Tephra: Materials of all types and sizes that are erupted from a crater or volcanic vent and deposited from the air.

Tremor: Low amplitude, continuous earthquake activity often associated with magma movement.

Tsunami: A great sea wave produced by a submarine earthquake, volcanic eruption, or large landslide.

Vent: The opening at the earth's surface through which volcanic materials issue forth.

Volcano: A vent in the surface of the Earth through which magma and associated gases and ash erupt; also, the form or structure (usually conical) that is produced by the ejected material.

Volcanic Arc: A generally curved linear belt of volcanoes above a subduction zone, and the volcanic and plutonic rocks formed there.

Volcanic Complex: A persistent volcanic vent area that has built a complex combination of volcanic landforms.

Vulcanian: A type of eruption consisting of the explosive ejection of incandescent fragments of new viscous lava, usually in the form of blocks.

Weathering: The process whereby exposed surface rocks are broken down by the effects of rain, frost, wind, and other elements of the weather. Weathering takes place on the spot, and does not involve any movement of the broken-down rock (erosion).

Adapted from the Volcano World website and SETI.

Selected References

Alford, Allen, *The Phoenix Solution*, Hodder and Stoughton, London, 1998.

Aliki, *Mummies Made in Egypt*, Harper Collins, 1979.

Bagavad-Gita: The Song of God, New Ameican Libray, 1951

Barber and Barber, *When They Severed Earth from Sky: How the Human Mind Shapes Myth*, Princeton University Press, 2004.

Barrow, John D., *Theories of Everything*, Oxford University Press, 1991

Bauval, Robert, and Gilbert, Adrian, *The Orion Mystery*, Crown, NY, 1994.

Berlitz, Charles, *The Mystery of Atlantis*, Avon, NY, 1976.

Blavatsky, H. P., *The Secret Doctrine: The Synthesis of Science, Religion, and Philosophy*, Theosophical Publishing, London, 1888.

Bower, B., "Human Origins Recede in Australia," Science News, Vol. 150, Sep. 28, 1996.

Brace, C. Loring, Nelson, Harry, and Korn, Noel, *Atlas of Fossil Man*, Holt, Rinehart and Winston, NY, 1971.

Brander, Bruce, *The River Nile*, National Geographic Society, 1966, 1968.

Browder, Anthony T., *Nile Valley Contributions to Civilization*, The Institute of Karmic Guidance, Washington, 1992.

Brunhouse, Robert L. *In Search of the Maya: The First Archeologists*, University of New Mexico Press, 1973.

Budge, E. A. Wallis, *An Egyptian Hieroglyphics Dictionary*, 2 vols., Dover, NY, 1978.

Budge, E. A. Wallis, *Egyptian Language*, Dover, NY, 1983.

Budge, E.A.Wallis, *Osiris and the Egyptian Resurrection*, 2 vols., Dover, NY, 1973 (1911 original).

Budge, E.A.Wallis, translator, *The Book of the Dead*, University Books, NY, 1960 (copy of 1913 Medici Society version).

Carey, S. Warren, *Theories of the Earth and Universe*, Stanford University Press, 1988.

Casti, John, *Paradigms Lost*, Avon Books, NY, 1989.

Cavendish, Richard, ed., *Mythology: An Illustrated Encyclopedia*, Barnes and Noble Books, 1993.

Cernan, C. W., *Gods, Graves, and Scholars*, Bantam, NY, 1972 (originally published in German in 1949).

Clark, R. T. Rundle, *Myth and Symbol in Ancient Egypt*, Thames and Hudson, NY, 1959.

Coe, Michael, *Breaking the Mayan Code*, Thames and Hudson, NY, 1992.

Cone, Joseph, *Fire Under the Sea*, William Morrow, NY, 1991.

Crick, Francis, *The Astonishing Hypothesis: The Scientific Search for the Soul*, Scribners, 1994.

Dalton, Bill, *Indonesian Handbook*, Moon Publications, Chico, California.

Darwin, Charles, *The Origin of Species*, Avenel Books, 1859.

Davidovits, Dr. Joseph, and Morris, Margie, *The Pyramids: An Enigma Solved*, Dorset Press, NY, 1988.

De Leeuw, *Crossroads of the Java Sea*, Jonathon Cape and Harrison Smith, NY 1931,

de Neve, G.A., "Earlier Eruptive Activities of Krakatau in Historic Time During the Quaternary," in Symposium on 100 Years Development of Krakatau and Its Surroundings, Volume I, LIPA, 1983.

Selected References

de Santillana, Giorgio, and von Dechend, Hertha, *Hamlet's Mill: An essay on myth and the frame of time.* Gambit, Boston, 1969.

Encyclopedia Britannica, William Benton, Chicago, 1952.

Encyclopedia Britannica, William Benton, Chicago, 1969.

Erman, Adolf, *Life in Ancient Egypt,* Dover Publications, NY, 1894, 1971.

Fagan, Brian, *The Journey from Eden,* Thames and Hudson Ltd., London, 1990.

Fagan, Brian, *Time Detectives,* Simon and Schuster, NY, 1995.

Feder, Kenneth, *Frauds, Myths, and Mysteries,* Mayfield Publishing, Mountain View, CA, 1996.

Feynman, Richard P., *Six Easy Pieces,* Helix Books, 1995.

Francis, Peter, *Volcanoes,* Penguin, 1976.

Freud, Sigmund, *Moses and Monotheism,* Vintage Books, 1939.

Furhman, Joel, M.D., *Fasting and Eating for Health,* St. Martin's Press, 1995.

Furneaux, Rupart, *Krakatau,* Prentice-Hall, Inc. NJ, 1964.

Fuller, R. Buckminster, *Critical Path,* St. Martin's, NY, 1981.

Fuller, R. Buckminster, *Tetrascroll,* St. Martin's, NY, 1975, 1982.

Galileo, *Dialog Concerning the Two New Sciences,* Great Books of the Western World, 1952 (originally 1638).

Gardener, Martin, *Fads and Fallacies in the Name of Science,* Dover, NY, 1954, 1957.

Gaulin, J. C. and McBurney, Donald, *Psychology: An Evolutionary Approach,* Prentice Hall,2001.

Gaulin, Steven J. C., McBurney, Donald H., *Evolutionary Psychology,* Second Edition, Pearson Prentice Hall, 2004

Godwin, Malcolm, *Angels: An Endangered Species,* Simon and Schuster, NY, 1990.

Greene, Mott T., *Natural Knowledge in Preclassical Antiquity,* Johns Hopkins, Baltimore, 1992.

Grove, Noel, "Volcanoes: Crucibles of Creation," *National Geographic,* Dec., 1992.

Harris, Stephan L., *Agents of Chaos: Earthquakes, Volcanoes and other Natural Disasters,* Mountain Press, Montana, 1990.

Haught, John F., *Responses to 101 Questions on God and Evolution,* Paulist Press, 2001

Hawking, Steven, *A Brief History of Time,* Bantam Books, 1988.

Hawkins, Jeff, *On Intelligence,* Times Books, 2004.

Heggie, Douglas, *Megalithic Science,* Thanmes and Hudson, 1981.

Herodotus, *The Histories,* Penguin Classics, 1972.

Horgan, John, *Rational Mysticism,* Houghton Mifflin, 2003

Hostetter, Clyde, *Star Trek to Hawa-ii, Mesopotamia to Hawa-ii,* The Diamond Press, CA, 1991.

Hutton, Peter, *Java,* Apa Productions, Hong Kong, 1980.

Islam: Muhammad and His Religion, Jeffery, ed., LAP, 1958.

Keys, David, *Catastrophe: An Investigation into the Origins of the Modern World,* Ballintine Books, 1999.

Kohler, Pierre, *Volcanoes and Earthquakes,* Barron's, NY, 1986.

Krafft, Maurice and Katia, *Volcanoes: Earth's Awakening,* Hammond, 1980.

Kuhn, Thomas, *The Structure of Scientific Revolutions,* University of Chicago Press, 1962.

LaMoreaux, Dr. Phillip E., and Idris, Col Hussein, *The Exodus: Myth, Legend, History,* Word Way Press, Alabama, 1996.

LaMoreaux, Philip, and Idris, *Hussein, The Exodus: Myth, Legend, History,* Word Way Press, Tuscaloosa, Alabama, 1996.

140

Selected References

Larick, Roy, and Ciochon, Russell, "The African Emergence and Early Dispersals of the Genus Homo," *American Scientist*, Vol. 84, No. 6, Nov-Dec 1996.

Le Plongeon, *Augustus, Queen Moo and the Egyptian Sphinx*, Health Research, Mokelumne Hill, CA, 1972.

Leeming, David Adams, *The World of Myth*, Oxford University Press, 1990.

Lehner, Mark, *The Complete Pyramids*, Thames and Hudson, London, 1997.

Luce, J. V., *The End of Atlantis*, Bantam, 1978.

Mackenzie, Donald A., *Pre-Columbian America: Myths and Mysteries*, Senate, NY, 1996.

Malinowski, Bronislav, *Magic, Science, and Religion*, Doubleday, 1948.

Margulis, Lyn, and Sagan, Dorian, *Acquiring Genomes*, Basic Books, 2003.

Marshall, Andrew and Walker, Zeanne, "Climbing the Tree of Life," *Garuda*, 1997.

Maspero, G., *New Light on Ancient Egypt*, Appleton and Co., NY, 1909.

McBride, L. R., *The Kahuna: Versatile Mystics of Old Hawaii*, Petroglyph Press, Hilo, Hawaii, 1983.

Melville, Leinani, *Children of the Rainbow*, Quest, 1969.

Mercer, Samuel A.B., *The Pyramid Texts*, Longmans, Green and Co., NY, 1952.

Michanowsky, George, *The Once and Future Star*, Barnes and Noble, NY, 1979.

Morgan, Elaine, *The Aquatic Ape*, Stein and Day, NY, 1982.

Morgan, Elaine, *The Scars of Evolution*, Oxford University Press, NY, 1990.

Oey, Eric M., editor, *Sumatra: Island of Adventure*, Passport Books, Lincolnwood, Chicago, 1996.

Oppenheimer, Steven, *Eden in the East: The Drowned Continent of Southeast Asia*, Orion, 1998.

Pauling, Linus, *College Chemistry*, Freeman, 1964.

Pellegrino, Charles, *Unearthing Atlantis*, Vintage Books, NY, 1991.

Pinker, Steven, *The Language Instinct*, Harper Perennial, 1995.

Pinker, Steven, *How the Mind Works*, W. W. Norton, 1999

Plato, Timaeus and Critias, 360 BC, translated by Benjamin Jowett, in *Great Books of the Western World*, Encyclopedia Britannica, William Benton, Chicago, 1952.

Powers, William, *Behavior: The Control of Perception*, 1973.

Pucci, Idanna, *Bhima Swarga: The Balinese Journey of the Soul*, Little, Brown and Company.

Quirke, S and Spencer, J., ed., *The British Museum Book of Ancient Egypt*, Thames and Hudson, 1992, 1996.

Ramage, Edwin, (ed.), *Atlantis: Fact or Fiction?* Indiana University Press, Bloomington, 1978.

Sagan, Carl, *The Demon-Haunted World*, Ballentine Books, 1996.

Sanders, N.K., *The Epic of Giglamesh*, Penguin, NY, 1960.

Schoch, Robert, *Voyages of the Pyramid Builders: The True Origins of the Pyramids from Lost Egypt to Ancient America*, Putnam, 2003.

Schwartz, Jean-Michel, *The Mysteries of Easter Island*, Avon, NY, 1973.

Sellers, Jane, *The Death of Gods in Ancient Egypt*, Penguin, London, 1992.

Shermer, Michael, *The Science of Good and Evil*, Times Books, 2004.

Simpkin, Tom and Fiske, Richard, *Krakatau 1883: The Volcanic Eruption and its Effects*, Smithsonian Institute Press, Washington DC, 1983.

Smith, Huston, *The Religions of Man*, Harper Collins Publishers, January 1965.

Smith, Huston, *Why Religion Matters*, Harper, SF, 2000.

Sobel, Dava, *Galileo's Daughter*, Penguin, 2000.

Stanford Encyclopedia of Philosophy, "Popper, Karl," Stanford University, (available online).

Selected References

Steiner, Rudolf, *Egyptian Myths and Mysteries*, Anthroposophic Press, NY, 1971.

The Epic of Gilgamesh, Penguin Classics, 1957.

The Upanishads: Breath of the Eternal, New American Library, 1957.

Thompson, Richard L., *Alien Identities*, Govardhan Hill, Alachua, Florida, 1993.

Thornton, Ian, *Krakatau: The Destruction and Reassembly of an Island Ecosystem*, Harvard University Press, Cambridge, 1996.

Tylor, Edward B., *Origins of Culture*, Peter Smith, Mass., 1970. (Originally published as Vol.1 of *Primitive Culture*, John Murray, London, sec. ed., 1873.)

Tylor, Edward B., *Primitive Culture*, Vol. I & II, John Murray, London, third ed., 1891.

Tylor, Edward B., *Religion in Primitive Culture*, Peter Smith, Mass., 1970. (Originally published as Vol.2 of *Primitive Culture*, John Murray, London, sec. ed., 1873.)

Vercoutter, Jean, *The Search for Ancient Egypt*, Harry Abrams, NY, 1992.

Vitaliano, D. B., *Legends of the Earth: Their Geological Origins*, Indiana University Press, Bloomington, 1973.

Volcano, Time-Life Editors, Time-Life Books, 1982.

Wasserman, James, *Egyptian Book of the Dead*, Raymond Faulkner, translator, Chronicle Books, San Francisco, 1994.

West, John Anthony, *Serpent in the Sky*, Quest Books, Wheaton, Illinois, USA, 1993 (Harper and Row, 1979)

Wilson, David Sloan, *Darwin's Cathedral*, University of Chicago Press, 2003.

Wilson, E. O., *Sociobiology: The New Synthesis*, Harvard University Press, 1975.

Wilson, Forbes, *The Conquest of Copper Mountain*, Antheneum, NY, 1981.

Wolpoff, Milford and Caspari, Rachel, *Race and Human Evolution*, Simon and Schuster, NY, 1997.

Zauzich, Karl-Theodor, *Hieroglyphs Without Mystery*, (Trans. Ann Macy Roth) University of Texas Press, 1992.

ENDNOTES: THE INVENTION OF GOD

1 Such as James Frazer's twelve volume classic, *The Golden Bough*.

2 Wilson, David Sloan, *Darwin's Cathedral*, p. 149.

3 Alford, Allen, *The Phoenix Solution*, Hodder and Stoughton, London, 1998.

4 Although there is some dispute about the origin of this word, I can understand why some etymologists are confused with "fire in the middle" as they see no connection between fire and pyramids, and so look for other possibilities. See *The Project Gutenberg EBook of New Word-Analysis*, by William Swinton. Pyrotechnic, funeral pyre, pyromania

5 *Skeptic* magazine, I don't recall which issue.

6 Larick, Roy, and Ciochon, Russell, "The African Emergence and Early Dispersals of the Genus Homo," American Scientist, Vol. 84, No. 6, Nov-Dec 1996.

7 Fagan, Brian, *Floods, Famines, and Emperors,* 1999, quoted by Calvin at http://williamcalvin.com/BrainForAllSeasons/Sahara.htm

8 LaMoreaux, Dr. Phillip E., and Idris, Col Hussein, *The Exodus: Myth, Legend, History*, Word Way Press, Alabama, 1996.

9 http://volcano.und.nodak.edu/vwdocs/volc_images/europe_west_asia/santorini.html

10 as told by Casti, p. 39.

11 Budge, *The Book of the Dead*, Chapter 146.

12 Budge, *The Book of the Dead*, Chapter 14.

13 de Neve, G.A., "Earlier Eruptive Activities of Krakatau in Historic Time During the Quaternary," in *Symposium on 100 Years Development of Krakatau and Its Surroundings*, Volume I, LIPA, 1983.

14 Thornton, Ian, *Krakatau: The Destruction and Reassembly of an Island Ecosystem*, Harvard University Press, Cambridge, 1996.

15 Clark, p. 37.

16 Budge, *The Book of the Dead*, Chapter 93.

17 Chapter 17, from http://www.sas.upenn.edu/African_Studies/Books/Papyrus_Ani.html,

18 Clark, p. 56.

19 Wasserman, Chapter 151.

20 Wasserman, Chapter 110.

21 Wasserman, *The Theban Recension*, p.122.

22 Budge, *Book of the Dead*, Chapter 156.

23 Mercer, Samuel A.B., *The Pyramid Texts*, Longmans, Green and Co., NY, 1952.

24 Budge, *Osiris and the Egyptian Resurrection*. Vol. 1, p. 1

25 Wasserman, Plate 2.

26 Budge, *Book of the Dead,* Chapter 1.

27 Wasserman, Plate 6.

28 Wasserman, Plate 11.

29 Wasserman, p.106.

30 Wasserman, Plate 33.

31 Wasserman, p. 111.

Endnotes

[32] From Volcanic World web site: http://volcano.und.nodak.edu/vwdocs/volc_images/img_erta_ale.html
"Erta Ale is a shield volcano in the Afar region of East Africa. Erta Ale is a remote and rarely visited volcano that is known currently to have an active lava lake in its summit crater. Erta Ale has undergone seven eruption events in the past 125 years. Three of the early eruption dates, 1873, 1903, and 1904 are uncertain. However, 1906, 1940, 1960, and 1967 are well established events. Erta Ale has been erupting continuously since 1967. Two new studies on Erta Ale have recently been published. Oppenheimer and Francis (1998) looked at the implications of long-lived lava lakes. They believe that Erta Ale's lava lake has been active for at least the last 90 years (making it one of the longest known historic eruptions)."

[33] Wasserman, Chapter 24, Plate 15.

[34] Budge, *Book of the Dead*, Chap. 175.

[35] There are images of these are the Internet.

[36] Budge, *Book of the Dead*, Chapter 151.

[37] http://www.thekeep.org/~kunoichi/kunoichi/themestream/wadjet.html

[38] Greene, p. 62.

[39] From Volcanic World website: Gilbert, J.S., and Lane, S. J., 1994, Electrical phenomena in volcanic plumes, in Casadevall, T.J., ed., *Volcanic ash and aviation safety: Proceedings of the first International Symposium on Volcanic Ash and Aviation Safety*: U.S. Geological Survey Professional paper 2047, p. 31-38.

[40] From Volcano World website: It has also been suggested that the charge is generated as the particles formed by fragmentation, not by collisions in the plume. Gilbert, J.S., and Lane, S. J., 1994, Electrical phenomena in volcanic plumes, in Casadevall, T.J., ed., *Volcanic ash and aviation safety: Proceedings of the first International Symposium on Volcanic Ash and Aviation Safety*: U.S. Geological Survey Professional paper 2047, p. 31-38.

[41] Greene, p.63.

[42] Greene, p. 61-62.

[43] Greene, p.63

[44] Mercer, p. 29.

[45] Budge, *Osiris and the Egyptian Resurrection*, Vol. 1, p.2

[46] Chapter 39, quoted by Clark, p. 211.

[47] Wasserman, Plate 14.

[48] Druitt, T.H., and Francaviglia, V., 1992, "Caldera formation on Santorini and the physiography of the islands in the late Bronze Age," *Bulletin of Volcanology*, v.54, p. 484-493. as quoted at http://volcano.und.nodak.edu/vwdocs/volc_images/europe_west_asia/santorini.html

[49] Wasserman, p. 113.

[50] Wasserman, p. 113

[51] Thornton, p. 28-39.

[52] Greene, p. 60.

[53] Furneaux, p. 113.

[54] Clark, p. 21.

[55] Lichtheim, *Ancient Egyptian Literature*, Vol. II, p. 215. Quoted by Sellers, p. 58.

[56] Coffin Texts III, 343, quoted by Clark, p. 225.

[57] quoted by Budge, *Osiris and the Egyptian Resurrection*, Vol. I, p. 62.

[58] Budge, *Book of the Dead*, Chapter 17.

[59] Budge, *Osiris and the Egyptian Resurrection*, Vol. 1, p. 86.

[60] Budge, *Osiris and the Egyptian Resurrection*, Vol. 1, p. 88

[61] Budge, *Osiris and the Egyptian Resurrection*, Vol. 1, p. 71.

[62] Wasserman, p. 134.

Endnotes

[63] Vitaliano, p. 164.

[64] Wasserman, p. 162.

[65] Wasserman, Plate 12-14.

[66] Wasserman, Plate 29.

[67] http://www.uwm.edu/Course/egypt/274RH/Texts/The%20Memphite%20Theology.htm

[68] Random House Webster's Unabridged Dictionary, 1999

[69] http://www.swagga.com/ankh.htm

[70] Greene. p. 57.

[71] The Stromboli volcano in Italy had periodic eruptions which would make it a good candidate for study by early humans. In fact, the word strombolian has come to describe a volcano that has frequent, moderate eruptions.

[72] Godwin, 1990, p. 24.

[73] Krafft, p. 11.

[74] New International Version available at: www.biblegateway.com

[75] New International Version available at: www.biblegateway.com

[76] all from www.biblegateway.com

[77] New International Version available at: www.biblegateway.com

[78] Fuller, 1981, p. 21.

[79] Although Freud has been criticized frequently in the last few decades, I predict that 500 years from now his books will still be read, while his critics will be long forgotten. Freud is certainly wrong in a number of instances, but such "pioneers" cannot be expected to achieve the same level of rigorousness as the later "settlers." In fact, it is these settlers that are expected to provide the rigor. The pioneers get the arrows, the settlers get the land.

[80] Freud, 1939, p. 39

[81] See Wikipedia, "The Historicity of Jesus."

[82] Do an Internet search. Many news sites reported this.

[83] Greene, p. 56.

[84] http://volcanoes.usgs.gov/Hazards/Effects/Ash+Aircraft.html

[85] quoted by Richard Thompson in *Alien Identities*, p. 265.

[86] http://www.mythome.org/RamaSummary.html

[87] summary by Dr. C. S. Shah, http://www.geocities.com/neovedanta/ramayana23.html

[88] for the next several paragraphs I rely on this book. *Mythology*, ed. by Cavendish, p. 17-19.

[89] http://www.sacred-texts.com/hin/rigveda/rv09018.htm

[90] http://www.sacred-texts.com/hin/rigveda/rv09019.htm

[91] http://www.sacred-texts.com/hin/rigveda/rv09018.htm

[92] Random House Dictionary

[93] http://www.jyh.dk/indengl.htm#Mandala

[94] http://www.newdawnmagazine.com/articles/mystery_of_shambhala_part_one.html

[95] http://www.shambhala.com/html/about/definition.cfm/

[96] http://www.ycsi.net/users/reversespins/agnishambhala.html

[97] Browder, p. 215.

[98] Schoch, 2003, p. 59.

[99] http://www.homestead.com/summoningspirit/AZTEC.html

[100] http://www.pacaritambo.com/deity.html

[101] http://www.scns.com/earthen/other/seanachaidh/godaztec.html

[102] www.encyclopedia.com/html/T/Tezcatli.asp

[103] http://home.iprimus.com.au/lunetta/index-32.html

Endnotes

[104] http://www.deliriumsrealm.com/delirium/mythology/tlaltecuhtli.asp

[105] http://weber.ucsd.edu/~anthclub/quetzalcoatl/que.htm

[106] http://weber.ucsd.edu/~anthclub/quetzalcoatl/que.htm

[107] http://frontpage2000.nmia.com/~nahualli/Quetzalcoatl/Elements/Clothing.htm

[108] They were killed while studying the volcanoes they loved.

[109] *Volcanoes: Earth's Awakening*, Katia and Maurice Krafft, Hammond, 1980, p. 31.

[110] *Mythology*, ed. by Cavendish, p. 59.

[111] *Parabola*, "Repaying Hun-tun's Kindness" Chinese, retold by Rama Devagupta," Fall 2003

[112] http://www.survive2012.com/dragons4.html#15

[113] *The World of Myth*, David Adams Leeming, p. 86-87

[114] de Santillana, Giorgio, and von Dechend, Hertha, *Hamlet's Mill*, p. 161.

[115] Greene, p.65.

[116] quoted by Greene, p. 68.

[117] quoted by Greene, p. 70.

[118] quoted by Greene, p. 70.

[119] Greene, p. 70-71.

[120] http://www.bulfinch.org/fables/bull2.html

[121] Strabo, 11.5.5 as quoted at: www.theoi.com/Ouranos/Prometheus.html

[122] http://oaks.nvg.org/oma.html#a32

[123] http://www.in2greece.com/english/historymyth/mythology/names/chimera.htm

[124] http://www.usd.edu/erp/Lycia/lycplace.html

[125] excerpted from *Meteorites in History* by John G. Burke (University of California Press, 1986), at http://www.alaska.net/~meteor/legend.htm

[126] Oppenheimer, p. 320-321.

[127] Oppenheimer, p. 322.

[128] I learned several things from this book including naturalistic explanations for the Arthurian sword legend, vampires, dwarfs, cattle mutilations, and the Centaur.

[129] quoted in Oppenheimer, p. 329, from Van Over, Raymond, *Sun Songs*, p. 137.

[130] Greene, p. 72.

[131] http://planetary.org/html/news/articlearchive/headlines/2003/neoworkshop.html

[132] http://www.noao.edu/meetings/mitigation/media/workshop_report.doc

[133] http://www.geology.sdsu.edu/how_volcanoes_work/Pelee.html

[134] http://www.geology.sdsu.edu/how_volcanoes_work/Pelee.html

[135] http://www.orientalarchitecture.com/yogyakarta/prambananindex.htm

[136] Vitaliano, p. 26.

[137] Keys, p. 277.

[138] Of course, there is also the threat of global warming. When I first started writing this book, many years ago, global warming wasn't as accepted as it is today.

[139] This list includes, but is not limited to: Abraham, Moses, Buddha, Pythagoras, Socrates, Plato, Aristotle, Zarathushtra, Jesus, Mohammed, Confucius, Lao Tse, Siyyid 'Ali-Muhammad, Madame Blavatsky, Krishnamurti, Mary Baker Eddy, Ellen G. White, Joseph Smith, Gandhi, Billy Graham, Sun Myung Moon, the Pope, the Dali Lama, Maharishi Mahesh Yogi, Carlos Casdaneda, Edgar Cayce, Rudolf Steiner, and L. Ron Hubbard.

[140] Tylor, Edward B., *Primitive Culture*, Vol. I & II, John Murray, London, third ed., 1891, 5-6.

[141] This is known as the "separatist approach." See Gould, Steven J., *Rock of Ages*, Ballentine Books, 1999.

[142] *Random House Webster's Unabridged Dictionary*, 1999, CD-Rom edition.

Endnotes

[143] *Random House Dictionary of the English Language*, print edition.

[144] Bower, B., "Human Origins Recede in Australia," *Science News*, Vol. 150, Sep. 28, 1996.

[145] Pauling, Linus, *General Chemistry*.

[146] see http://www.swil.ocdsb.edu.on.ca/FreRev/lavois.html and also, http://www.woodrow.org/teachers/ci/1992/Lavoisier.html

[147] see http://www.swil.ocdsb.edu.on.ca/FreRev/lavois.html

[148] http://www.brainyencyclopedia.com/encyclopedia/c/cr/cremation.html

[149] Freud, 1939, p. 146.

[150] *Sociobiology: The New Synthesis*, p. 561

[151] www.workreference.com

[152] http://www.wmich.edu/dialogues/themes/indianwords.htm

[153] http://www.wmich.edu/dialogues/themes/indianwords.htm

[154] http://www.etymonline.com/index.html

[155] http://www.storytellingmonk.org/downloads/metaphorical_meaning_sanskrit_terms.pdf

[156] Although I can think of science fiction scenarios of people sending their corpses into space.

[157] http://www.clas.ufl.edu/users/gthursby/taoism/ttcstan3.htm#13 A Translation by Stan Rosenthal.

[158] http://www.san.beck.org/Laotzu.html#51

[159] http://www.chemeng.ucl.ac.uk/research/combustion/nl2003_1/nl03_110.html

[160] http://www.tenspeedpress.com/whatsnew/page.php3?ftr=126

[161] http://angelreiki.nu/reiki/ReikiGlossary.htm

[162] http://holisticonline.com/Reiki/hol_Reiki_home.htm

[163] Prana-Vyana-Samana-Apana-Udana, from *The Mahabharata*, Santi Parva Section CLXXXIV at: http://www.hinduism.co.za/prana-vy.htm

[164] Vivekananda, Swami, *Raja Yoga*, pp. 29, 30. quoted at: http://beaskund.helloyou.ws/netnews/bk/soul/soul1028.html

[165] www.hyperdictionary.com

[166] Random House Webster's CD-Rom version.

[167] http://uwacadweb.uwyo.edu/religionet/er/hinduism/HGLOSSRY.HTM

[168] http://hinduwebsite.com/hinduism/h_maya.htm

[169] http://classics.mit.edu/Plato/timaeus.html

[170] http://www.hellenism.net/eng/soul_literature.htm

[171] Random House Dictionary of the English Language.

[172] Davidovits, glossary.

[173] Clark, p. 232-233.

[174] Random House Dictionary of the English Language.

[175] *Ptahhotep*, ed. Devaud, 1.135ff. as quoted in Clark p. 231.

[176] *Ptahhotep*, ed. Devaud, 1.135ff. as quoted in Clark p. 232.

[177] Budge, 1960, p. 75.

[178] Budge, 1960, p. 73.

[179] Quoted in Budge, 1960, p. 74.

[180] Budge, 1960, p. 76.

[181] Random House Dictionary of the English Language.

[182] Crick, 1994, p. 3

Endnotes

[183] To find life like ours on extrasolar planets, planets that do not orbit the Home Star, we can use oxygen in the atmosphere as a marker. James Lovelock pioneered this method when looking for life on Mars. He told NASA we didn't need to go there because of the atmospheric composition of Mars. In the future, 20-60 years, we may discover life near other stars using this method.

[184] "The Rise of Oxygen," by Lee J. Siegal, *Astrobiology Magazine*, at: http://www.astrobio.net/news/article541.html

[185] "The Rise of Oxygen," by Lee J. Siegal, *Astrobiology Magazine*, at: http://www.astrobio.net/news/article541.html

[186] Marsh and Crawford, p. 67.

[187] Marsh and Crawford, p. 68.

[188] Many people feel that their pets love them unconditionally. I think pets love us on the condition that we feed them unconditionally.·

[189] Random House Dictionary of the English Language.

[190] Furhman, 1995.

[191] Of course, this will never be popular with the advertising-controlled media. Drug companies, also known as Big Pharma, would lose too much money if fasting were to become popular

[192] To read more about this, get Gary Cziko's book *The Things We Do*.

[193] A philosophy closely related to what I have been discussing is what's known as "logical positivism." A central tenet of logical positivism is that metaphysical, theological, and ethical sentences are "cognitively meaningless."

[194] Hawkins, *On Intelligence*.

[195] Korzybski, "Science and Sanity."

[196] Even twins reared together have different experiences. When they play cards together and one wins and the other loses, they have somewhat opposite experiences.

[197] Feynman, *Six Easy Pieces*, p. 4.

[198] Worship originally meant "worth-ship" or a condition of worth. It probably had a meaning similar to that of "respect" today.

[199] It is possible that the *search for oxygen* and *dreams* somehow worked together to create "spirits" or "souls" and even "Gods" or "God".

[200] Margulis and Sagan, *Acquiring Genomes*, 2003

[201] Speculating: during the next appearance of land bridges, the more human-like apes could have migrated back to the mainland, so that (perhaps) you have the *ice ages* operating in conjunction with a *volcanic evolutionary pump* 1) isolating, 2) forcing into the sea, 3) allowing migration to the mainland, 1) isolating, 2) forcing into the sea, 3) allowing migration to the mainland; a cyclical process, during successive ice ages, that eventually selected modern bipedal *Homo sapiens*. Thus, possibly each ice age, along with the appearance and disappearance of the land bridges, caused a newly mutated, better adapted human to be selected.

[202] I am following Bucky Fuller's thinking here which is developed in several of his books.

[203] Leinani Melville, author of *Children of the Rainbow*, Quest, 1969.

[204] See the book *The Pyramids: An Enigma Solved* by Dr. Davidovits and M. Morris for a fuller explanation of the synthesis of artificial stone, or geopolymerization, by early humans. He also has a web site.

[205] See the video, *Ring of Fire: East of Krakatau*.

[206] Vitaliano, p. 196

[207] For example, the 1997 eruption of Popocatepetl, or Smoking Mountain, very near Mexico City.